# A Crash Course in Teaching Religion

MARY KATHLEEN GLAVICH, SND

# a CRASH COURSE in TEACHING RELIGION

TWENTY THIRD 23rd
PUBLICATIONS

# Dedication

To the people at St. Dominic Church,
Shaker Heights, Ohio,
who value religious education:
Father Tom Fanta, the parish staff,
and the parishioners,
especially the volunteer catechists

**Second printing 2006**

Twenty-Third Publications
A Division of Bayard
One Montauk Avenue, Suite 200
PO Box 6015
New London, CT 06320
(860) 437-3012 or (800) 321-0411
www.23rdpublications.com

ISBN-10: 1-58595-562-0
ISBN 978-1-58595-562-6

Library of Congress Catalog Card Number: 2005935873
Printed in the U.S.A.

# Table of Contents

# Introduction

*Go therefore and make disciples of all nations, baptizing them in the name of the Father and of the Son and of the Holy Spirit, and teaching them to obey everything that I have commanded you. (Matthew 28:19–20a)*

Some of us are called to carry out this comission from Jesus in a formal way by teaching religion to the next generation. This may be as a Catholic school teacher, a catechist in a parish school of religion, an instructor in family or community centered catechesis, or a parent who homeschools.

This is a guide for teaching religion in any of these roles. It concisely and simply presents the basics of a methods course for teaching religion and features ideas, lists of information, and tips that can be drawn on forever after. It is particularly geared to those who teach children in grades kindergarten through eight.

Each chapter opens with "centering," one or two questions or an exercise that enables the reader to zero in on the topic, usually by recalling personal experiences. At the end of each chapter, Ways to Respond are suggested so the reader can apply what was learned. These two features are especially helpful when the book serves as a textbook in a catechetical methods course.

No matter whether we are experienced or quite green, whether we teach for a living, have volunteered to teach or have been "volunteered," we can always benefit from learning more about the fundamentals, techniques, and tricks of the trade.

For encouragement and strength while pursuing your role as teacher, keep in mind the promise Jesus made at the end of his commission: "Remember, I am with you always" (Matthew 28:20b).

# 1

# *Called to Teach*

*Why are you a religion teacher?*
*Who was your best religion teacher? Why?*

The future of the Church and the world is in your hands. The next generation will not know Jesus and his teachings unless we today tell his story. This is the vital role and the special vocation (call) of the those who teach religion.

Catechesis is rooted in evangelization, which means spreading the good news. The term "catechist," used for someone who teaches religion, is from the Greek for "resound" or "echo." Through us the gospel echoes down through the ages. As we teach, we carry out the ministry of the word; and for this, Scripture praises us: "How beautiful are the feet of those who bring good news!" (Romans 10:15b). In Scripture's roster of church members, we rank third after apostles and prophets, but before miracle-workers and healers (1 Corinthians 12:28).

> Catechesis is that particular form of the ministry of the word which matures initial conversion to make it into a living, explicit, and fruitful confession of faith (*General Directory for Catechesis*, #82).

The content we transmit is God's word found in Scripture, Tradition, liturgy, and our experience of creation and life.

Our task is threefold: to have the faith penetrate the children's heads, touch their hearts, and move their hands to action.

*Head.* We want the children to know the faith as taught by the Church, the faith in its entirety.

*Heart.* We also want them to accept the faith, cherish it, and adopt its values.

*Hands.* Finally, we want them to live the faith, especially through loving service.

## ✎ Tip

Recall what St. Francis of Assisi advised a brother sent to preach to a town: "Preach, and if necessary use words."

Our work has been delegated to us. Handing on the Catholic faith to children is primarily their parents' role. We teachers are merely parents' assistants, a truth to clarify for them whenever possible. Teaching, ruling, and sanctifying are the three main jobs of bishops. As religion teachers we share in our bishop's teaching ministry and represent him as well.

Here's a challenging thought: we teach by example. You are your students' model of what it means to be a Catholic Christian, a follower of Jesus Christ. Pope Paul VI once observed that people today listen more willingly to witnesses than to teachers, and if they do listen to teachers, it is because they are witnesses.

In the ministry of catechetics we serve our students. We act as witness for them—ones who speak for God.

Although it goes without saying that teaching the Catholic Christian faith should be centered on Christ, the *Catechism of the Catholic Church,* in article 426, states it emphatically:

At the heart of catechesis we find, in essence, a Person, the Person of Jesus of Nazareth, the only Son from the Father.... who suffered and died for us and who now, after rising, is living with us forever. [To catechize is] to reveal in the Person of Christ the whole of God's eternal design reaching fulfillment in that Person. It is to seek to understand the meaning of Christ's actions and words and of the signs worked by him.

Catechesis aims at putting "people…in communion…with Jesus Christ: only he can lead us to the love of the Father in the Spirit and make us share in the life of the Holy Trinity."

## Characteristics of a Religion Teacher

According to the introduction in the *National Directory for Catechesis*, a religion teacher's spirituality:

- centers on an encounter with Christ
- is rooted in the living word of God
- fosters an abiding hope that all should come to the knowledge of the truth of Christ and accept salvation from him
- expresses itself in a sincere love for the Church in imitation of Christ
- seeks interior growth in the peace and joy of Christ
- embraces the Paschal Mystery
- enters into the apostolic mission of Christ, and
- is enriched by a deep devotion to the Mother of God.

It stands to reason that anyone who attempts to bring people to Jesus is a friend of his. A religion teacher cherishes and nurtures a good relationship with Jesus and his Church. This is manifested by a commitment to prayer, Scripture reading, and the Eucharist; an openness to the Spirit; a life in conformity with Catholic moral standards; and a desire to grow in understanding the faith.

What are other characteristics of an effective religion teacher? Here are some qualities we can look for:

| | |
|---|---|
| confident | patient |
| enthusiastic | open |
| consistent | generous |
| flexible | kind |
| tactful | compassionate |
| caring | forgiving |
| hopeful | cheerful |
| creative | |

A religion teacher needs two special senses:

1. Common sense
2. A sense of humor

Finally, a religion teacher should be able to communicate faith and knowledge effectively—or at least be open to taking training courses to learn how to do this.

## The Religion Teacher's Tasks

The *National Directory for Catechesis* identifies our main task as the formation of disciples of Jesus Christ. This includes the following six responsibilities of our ministry, which should all be carried out in a balanced way:

- sharing knowledge of the faith
- educating about liturgy (worship)
- providing moral formation
- showing how to pray
- instructing for community life, and
- promoting a missionary spirit (witness and service).

Underlying the success of these tasks, however, is a focus on what is at the heart of the vocation of the religion teacher: *bringing people closer to Jesus*!

## Requirements for Being a Religion Teacher

Most dioceses have a certification process that requires courses in faith, methods, and spirituality. Offered by the diocese or local colleges, these courses may also be taken through a video program or long-distance learning via the Internet. Once a basic certificate is obtained, it can be renewed by attending other courses, lectures, workshops, and conventions; or an advanced certificate can be pursued.

Training—such as that offered in the Virtus program—may also be required so that a teacher can recognize and prevent sexual abuse. Usually fingerprinting and background checks are expected, too.

## Dignity of the Teacher

As a religion teacher commissioned to carry on the teaching ministry of Jesus Christ, you have dignity. This role requires a certain professionalism. Here are ways not only to project a professional image but to give you credibility and show your students that you value them:

**✎ Tip**

Remember that in all your interactions with the students, you represent Jesus.

- Ask the students to call you by your title—Mr., Mrs., or Miss—not by your first name.
- Dress neatly and appropriately, a cut above what you wear around the house.
- Avoid sitting on desks (yours or the children's) while teaching.
- Do not eat, chew gum, or drink coffee while teaching.
- Watch your language!

Expect and demand that the students show you respect. When they don't, deal with it immediately.

## Ethics for a Religion teacher

Some guidelines for your moral behavior:

- Guard the children's reputation by not speaking to others about their faults.
- Speak respectfully to others about a child, especially, in front of the child.
- Use with discretion the information you know about children.
- Speak professionally about children, their parents, and their homes.
- Prepare lesson plans well.
- Seek help for children in need.
- Meet with a child at appropriate times and places. Never be alone with a child with the door closed.
- Aim to live the faith you teach.

## Professional Growth

Here are seven ways to broaden your understanding of your faith and ministry, stay updated, find new ideas for teaching, and keep alive your enthusiasm:

1. Take the required courses for certification.
2. Sit in on the classes of good religion teachers and discuss the lesson afterward with them.
3. Attend in-service sessions and meetings for religion teachers.
4. Go to national and diocesan conventions, conferences, and institutes related to religious education.
5. Read books and magazines on catechesis and faith.
6. Welcome the opportunity to be observed and evaluated, and accept constructive criticism from those qualified to offer it.
7. Pray and participate in the sacraments.

### Ways to Respond

• Draw an outline of a person. Add features to illustrate the characteristics of a religion teacher. For example, draw a large heart to show the love a teacher needs.

• Develop a score card to rate your attributes as a teacher. In which areas are you strongest? In which are you weakest?

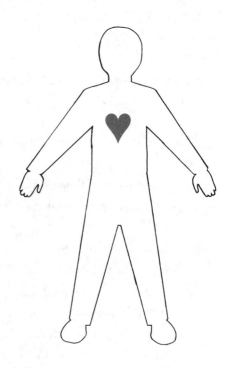

# 2

# *Your Students*

*When did a teacher's words or actions make you feel
good about yourself or serve to motivate you?
Have your words motivated your students?
How can you tell?*

Knowing your young Christians is a key to success. Each age has its own characteristics. Your manual might summarize these for you. People develop their powers in stages. Your manual's lesson plans and recommended materials are geared to your students' age and developmental level.

✎ **Tip**

Exchange letters. Ask your students to write you a letter about themselves. Also, write each one a handwritten note of introduction.

You get to know your students by interacting with them before and after class, at parish activities, through their answers in class, and by hearing their prayer intentions. Ask your children about their families, pets, sports, and hobbies. Listen to their concerns, ideas, stories, and gripes.

Think positively about your students. Don't let negative comments from previous teachers taint your image of them before you even meet them. Also, avoid comparing them unfavorably to your previous class. Your present class is a year younger than your former class was when they left you!

At dismissal time, stand at the door and say good-bye to the children. You might even bless each one.

## Names

As quickly as possible, learn your students' names and how to spell and pronounce them. Have the children wear name badges or give them name cards. Until you know the children, seat them in alphabetical order. To make your lessons personal, use the children's names as you teach. Call on the children by name. (Pointing to them is not as polite.) When appropriate, use their names in your examples and stories.

## Multiple Intelligences

Education professor Howard Gardner proposed that we do not have just the mental aptitude that IQ tests measure. He identified eight distinct intelligences. The way your students learn is linked to the type of intelligence they have. In your lessons incorporate activities that involve all the intelligences. Here are the eight ways to be smart and some learning activities that draw on them:

EIGHT FORMS OF INTELLIGENCE

*Linguistic:* Reading, storytelling, word games, writing, discussing

*Logical-Mathematical:* Board games, category and pattern activities, questions, problem solving, step-by-step presentations, analyzing and interpreting

*Musical:* Making and listening to music

*Spatial* (visual): Art, models, diagrams, maps, and pictures

*Bodily-Kinesthetic:* Motor skills, bodily movement, and hands-on activities

*Interpersonal:* Leadership and caring activities, role-play and drama, working in pairs or groups, team games, service projects, and celebrations

*Intrapersonal* (introspective): Debriefing learning activities, organizing, time for reflection, independent study, prayer, goal-setting, and self-evaluation

*Naturistic* (distinguishing flora and fauna, seeing patterns in nature, determining how nature affects civilization): Bringing in things from nature, getting involved in conservation projects, and creation-based prayer

## Learning Styles

Your students learn in one of three ways. It's said that

65% of people learn visually,

30% learn aurally, and

5% learn kinesthetically (tactilely).

Teachers tend to teach in their favorite style of learning. Try to identify how each of your students learns best and plan activities that match the needs of all.

## Expectations

Children tend to live up to your expectations. Therefore, by your words and actions, communicate that you expect them to pay attention, do their homework, remember to bring their books, etc. Conveying that you don't care or don't

> **✎ Tip**
>
> Treat the students as though they already were what you hope they become.

really think they will follow through allows children to settle for mediocrity—or worse! Keep your standards high. Remember that you are to facilitate your students' success.

## Motivation

Some children are intrinsically motivated to learn. They are curious and eager to achieve. Our job would be easy if all children loved to learn, but that is not the case. We are challenged to come up with creative ways to light the fire under them so they do the work of learning. Here are some ideas:

- Arouse the students' curiosity through the use of intriguing opening activities.

- Get them to ask questions about topics; make them ponder and wonder about things.
- Give out stickers, holy cards, balloons, bows, and certificates as rewards.

- Keep charts with stars or stickers for those who are present or those who have done homework.
- At the end of each lesson, award a badge with a safety pin on the back that says "Super Student," "Real 1st Grader," or "Star Disciple" to a child and explain why he or she deserves it. The child wears the badge home and must return it for the next class. (Have another one ready in case someone forgets.)
- At the beginning of class pin on a child a badge with a picture of Jesus to encourage that child to be a good disciple during class.
- Reserve a certain chair or job as a privilege for a good or improving student.
- Make your lessons enjoyable and fun.
- Be excited about what you teach.

## Hierarchy of Human Needs

Psychologist Abraham Maslow proposed a hierarchy of human needs that, when met, lead to self-actualization or maturity. Children are more likely to learn when these needs are met.

- Self-actualization
- Respect (self-esteem)
- Love (belongingness)
- Safety (security)
- Physical needs

## Affirmation

Children learn best when they have self-esteem. You can build it by these practices:

- Convey that their ideas have value.
- Display their work (and not just the best samples) in the classroom, the school hall, or the church lobby.
- Write positive comments on their work.
- Mail the students a complimentary note.
- Surprise parents with a call about a child's good work or progress.
- Accept responses to questions positively, even if the student answers incorrectly or can't answer. Use comments such as these: "Almost," "Not quite," "A good try, but that's not the answer." "Can someone help him (or her) out?"
- Offer a reason when praising someone. It will mean more.
- Use positive expressions like those listed below under "Words of Praise."
- Smile! (Someone has said a smile is a visual hug.)

## Words of Praise

Add some of these expressions to your "teacher vocabulary" to affirm a child who has answered correctly or has done good work:

| | |
|---|---|
| A-OK! | Dynamite! |
| Awesome! | Excellent. |
| Beautiful work. | Exceptional work. |
| Big improvement. | Fabulous. |
| Bravo! | Fantastic job. |
| Brilliant. | First-rate! |
| Clever. | Good for you. |
| Congratulations! | Good job. |
| Correct. | Good thinking. |
| Delightful. | Great idea. |

Great work.
Hip, hip hooray!
How smart.
Hurray for you.
I can count on you.
I knew you could do it.
I'm proud of you.
Impressive.
Improving.
Incredible.
Interesting.
Lovely.
Magnificent.
Marvelous.
A masterpiece.
Neat.
Nice job.
Nicely done.
Outstanding.
Phenomenal.
Remarkable.
Sensational.
Spectacular!
Splendid.
Super!

Swell!
Terrific.
Thank you for sharing.
Three cheers.
Top-notch.
Tremendous.
Unique.
Very creative.
Way to go!
Well done.
What a good listener.
Wonderful.
Wow!
Yes!
You are one in a million.
You are responsible.
You brighten my day.
You figured it out.
You have a great smile.
You made my day.
You tried hard.
You've got it.
You're a good helper.
You're a winner.
You're catching on.
You're fantastic.
You're incredible.
You're on target.
You're on your way.
You're so thoughtful.
You're special.
You're the best.
You're wonderful.
You should be proud.

**Tip**

For older students,
cut out positive
words from maga-
zines and newspa-
pers and glue them
to their papers.

## Reaching Out to All

Sometimes we're so wrapped up in teaching that unconsciously we call on the same students repeatedly while others are left to daydream—or get into trouble! Sometimes, when we're pressured to quickly get through a lesson, we're tempted to call on just those students who will have the right answer. Try to be aware of the "quiet" ones. Draw all students into the lesson by directing questions to them and by asking them to do things like erasing the board and passing out papers.

## Don't Touch

For your own protection, unless it is totally appropriate, avoid physical contact with your students so that you do not risk facing accusations of cruelty or sexual impropriety.

## Prayer for Students

Pray for the students during class (aloud and silently) as well as during your daily prayer. Keep a list of your students in your Bible or prayer book. One seasoned educator suggested, "We should talk more to God about our students than we talk to our students about God."

## Love

Let your children know you love them. Remember that the student who is most unlovable is probably the one who most needs love.

## Class Size

Fifteen is a good number of students for a religion class. If your class is much larger than this, you might ask if two classes can be formed. For big classes, secure an aide (perhaps a parent of one of your students) to help with routines and discipline.

> ✎ **Tip**
>
> If an extrovert or two take over your lessons with long stories, curtail their monologues with a gentle response such as, "I'd really like to hear about this. Could you tell me after class?"

## Multicultural Consciousness

Culture affects how people hear and respond to God's word. Moreover, we want our students to know about, respect, and cherish unique cultures. For these two reasons, it is important to integrate different cultures and traditions into our teaching, especially those of the children we teach. Here are suggestions for doing this:

- Choose pictures, books, and media that are inclusive of all cultures.
- When giving examples in lessons, draw on your knowledge of different ethnic customs.
- Learn about the history, traditions, and values of your children's ethnic groups.
- Be creative in making use of your students' backgrounds. For example, ask the children what traditions their families practice during Advent, Christmas, Lent, or Easter.
- Introduce saints and feasts that are special for particular cultures.
- Teach songs from different countries.
- Acknowledge the contributions of different cultures that enrich the traditions of the Church.

## Special Needs Children

Today children with special needs are mainstreamed. The registration form for your program should include a section for a parent to alert the teacher to their child's special needs. Catechists should look to their DRE for guidance in this regard.

A FEW GROUND RULES

1. Speak to the parents to learn more about the child.
2. For a child who needs much help in order to learn, ask for an aide (or the child's parent) to provide guidance during class.
3. Never embarrass a child or allow others to do so.
4. Involve the child as much as possible in interacting with the other children. Respecting the privacy of a student is sacrosanct.

It may be helpful to consult a professional about a particular disability. Also, you might want to discuss the child's Individualized Education Program (IEP) with your DRE or principal.

## HELP FOR CHILDREN WITH SPECIAL NEEDS

To teach special needs children about Jesus, some techniques are especially helpful. Actually many of these methods are effective for the rest of the class, too! Here are ideas for particular needs:

*Physical Disability*

- If there's no aide, assign another child to help with activities.
- Include the child in class activities in whatever way possible.
- Do your best to make the room safe for the child.
- Be certain that there is a plan in place should you need to evacuate during an emergency. This plan should not include only children. Rather, find out in advance whether there is another adult nearby who could lend a hand should there be a need.

*Visual Impairment*

- Seat the child where he or she can see best.
- Let the child move closer to see displayed items.
- Provide the child with large-print books and worksheets, audio materials, and tangible materials for use in the class and at home.
- Permit the child to do assignments and tests orally or to tape-record them.
- Assign a buddy to help with visual activities.
- Make sure the learning space is free from hazards for the child.

*Hearing Impairment*

- Seat the child in the front of the room and near audio equipment when you use it.
- If a child is impaired in one ear, seat him or her so the impaired ear faces the wall.
- Write directions on the board.
- Face the child when speaking to him or her and talk clearly.

- Give the child written copies of notes, scripts, stories, and other material presented orally in class.
- Use lots of visuals.

*Speech Impairment*
- Have an aide work individually with the child for oral tasks.
- Allow time for the child to respond to your questions (and make sure other students do not cut off him or her).

*Social and Behavioral Problems*
- Minimize distractions as much as possible.
- Keep to routines and avoid last-minute changes in the lesson.
- After a quiet activity, carry out one that is more active.
- Explain why the child is learning the topic.
- Propose a plan of action for assignments.
- Reward the child for completing a task in a given time.
- Use strategies with immediate feedback: e.g., hand raising and flashcards.

*Learning Disability*
- Seat the child near you.
- Keep to routines and avoid distractions.
- Plan short activities and review often.
- Use many pictures.
- Grade for content not writing and reading ability.
- Create situations in which the child will be successful.
- Compliment the child often on strengths, efforts, and successes.
- Keep instructions brief.
- Show, don't just tell, what the child is to do.
- Review and clarify directions. Have the child repeat them.
- Ask questions frequently to make sure the child understands.
- Capitalize on the skills the child has.
- Let the child finish work at home with parental help.

*Attention Deficit Hyperactivity Disorder (ADHD):* characterized by inattention, impulsivity, and hyperactivity. In addition to actions under "Learning Disability":

- For a hyperactive child, channel energy into acceptable activities.
- Draw attention to the child's good performance.
- Offer both oral and written instruction so the child is less likely to fail at completing in-class tasks or homework.
- Provide organization tools (check lists, folders, etc.).
- Gently bring the child back to task when his or her attention sags for more than a few minutes.
- Suggest ways to resolve a situation that may lead to conflict.
- Use variety in instruction.
- Reinforce interest in areas where the child is curious and enthusiastic.
- Find ways the child can help peers.

Many children with disabilities receive a great deal of negative feedback, so be quick to compliment them when they make the effort to complete their work.

*The Gifted*

- Suggest enrichment activities and supplementary resources.
- Enlist the child's help in class.
- Encourage high-level thinking skills by providing challenging and creative exercises.

### Ways to Respond

- Mentally review how much you know about each child in your class.
- Keep a list of your children's names in your prayer book.

# 3

# *Basic Tools*

*Leaf through your manual and find one helpful thing
you hadn't realized was there.
What features do you like best in your manual?*

Religion teachers have at their disposal a wealth of excellent materials designed to guide and support them. The challenge is carving out the time to implement these recommendations and tap into these resources.

## The Teacher's Manual

Your teacher's manual is your most important tool. Designed by experts in theology and religious education, these lessons present concepts on the students' level through activities that meet the whole range of learning styles. The lessons are also doctrinally sound and reflect current Church teaching. Catechetical materials are reviewed by a committee of three appointed by the United States Conference of Bishops to determine whether or not they are in conformity with the *Catechism of the Catholic Church*.

> ✎ **Tip**
>
> Write in your book. Before a lesson, add comments, highlight sections or phrases, and draw arrows. After a lesson, make notes that will help you next time you teach that lesson.

CURRICULUM

A religion series covers faith, sacraments, the Church, prayer, and Scripture in a comprehensive and systematic way. Certain topics will be stressed in the grade you are teaching. The religion teachers in the following years expect to build on the groundwork you lay. Your program may provide a scope and sequence chart, that is, an overview of everything that is taught in the series and in what grade it is covered. Look at this to see what your class has learned previously and what they will learn in the next grade.

**Tip**

When possible, ask parents to review parts of each lesson with their child and to sign off on these. This will help them remember to send the textbook back with their child.

LESSON PLANS

Your manual provides step-by-step lesson plans that present the material in words the children can understand. Explanations, questions, and activities all develop the topic, and the concepts are true to Church teaching. By following the manual, you know you are teaching the faith in an effective way for the children in your class. The plans usually offer alternate activities and resources to choose from so you can tailor your lesson to your children. They also include tips for teaching. It's wise to follow the plan as is until you have enough experience and knowledge to develop your own lessons.

RESOURCE SECTION

Your manual includes many helpful resources. Among other things, it may list characteristics of the children you teach, offer ideas for teaching children with special needs, and supply titles of books and audiovisual materials related to the topics.

## The Textbook

Your manual's lesson plan explains how to use to the optimum the book's text, activities, charts, art, and photos. Become familiar with the children's books. Know where the basic Catholic prayers and facts are. See if there is a glossary, an index, tear-out pages, and booklets to use throughout the year. Are there supplementary lessons in the back?

Ideally the children keep their books and write in them. Let the children take their books home for study, homework, and carrying out suggested family activities. If you insist that the children bring their books to class, they will. Be consistent with this.

Tell your students that because their religion books are about God, they should respect them by keeping them neat and clean and not doodling in them.

## The Resource Library

Your parish probably has a collection of books, magazines, CDs, DVDs, and videos for religious education. These are for your personal growth as a religion teacher and for use with your students. Browse through these and note which ones could be of use to you. Follow the procedure for taking them out.

You might want to start your own resource library at home.

---

### Ways to Respond

- Examine your manual and student book thoroughly, especially the front and back matter.
- Choose one optional activity from a lesson and try to individualize it as much as possible.

---

# 4

# *Resources*

*What Catholic Web sites are you familiar with?*
*Which have been most helpful to you?*

As a religion teacher you should own (and read!) a Bible and a copy of the *Catechism of the Catholic Church*.

## The Bible

The Bible is the word of God in the words of human beings. God is present in Scripture and speaks to us in a special way. Along with Tradition, the Bible comprises our "deposit of faith." It is the source of our knowledge about salvation history and our savior, Jesus Christ, whose life is presented in the four gospels. Pope Benedict XVI stated, "Only those who first listen to the Word can become preachers of it."

## The Catechism of the Catholic Church

The *Catechism* was first published in 1986; a revision appeared in 1992. Following a long tradition, the *Catechism* is divided into four parts to cover the pillars of Catholic belief: the creed, the sacred liturgy, the Christian way of life, and the prayer of Christians. In 2006, the U.S. bishops published the *Compendium of the Catechism of the Catholic Church*, a summary of the *Catechism* intended to be used as a reference.

# How the Four Pillars of the Catechism are Related

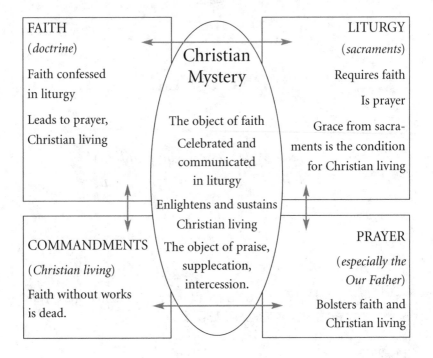

| FAITH | Christian Mystery | LITURGY |
|---|---|---|
| (*doctrine*) | | (*sacraments*) |
| Faith confessed in liturgy | The object of faith | Requires faith |
| Leads to prayer, Christian living | Celebrated and communicated in liturgy | Is prayer |
| | Enlightens and sustains Christian living | Grace from sacraments is the condition for Christian living |
| COMMANDMENTS | The object of praise, supplecation, intercession. | PRAYER |
| (*Christian living*) | | (*especially the Our Father*) |
| Faith without works is dead. | | Bolsters faith and Christian living |

## Other Resources

To help you, your parish resource center probably has other books, documents, and magazines such as the following.

### CONCORDANCE

A concordance is useful when you are searching for a particular Scripture verse or story. It lists words followed by all of the verses in the Bible that contain them.

### GENERAL DIRECTORY FOR CATECHESIS

Published by the Vatican in 1971 and revised in 1997, this book gives guidelines and directives for fostering the faith and aims to encourage religion teachers by nurturing hope.

## NATIONAL DIRECTORY FOR CATECHESIS

Published in 1979 and revised in 2005 by the United States Conference of Catholic Bishops, this reference book gives principles and guidelines for renewing catechesis in the United States. It explains the various components of catechesis.

## CHURCH DOCUMENTS

The popes and bishops have issued several documents on or related to catechesis. Some of these are the following:

- Pope Paul VI's *On Evangelization in the Modern World* (*Evangelii nuntiandi*) (1975), in which catechesis is defined as a work of evangelization in the context of the Church's mission
- Pope John Paul II's *On Catechesis in Our Time* (*Catechesi tradendae*) (1979), in which catechesis is called a remarkable moment in the whole process of evangelization
- the United States bishops' document *Our Hearts Were Burning within Us* about adult education, *To Teach as Jesus Did* (1972), and *Basic Teachings for Catholic Religious Education* (1973)
- the sixteen documents of the Second Vatican Council.

## MAGAZINES/NEWSLETTERS FOR RELIGION TEACHERS

You or your religious education office might subscribe to *RTJ: The Magazine for Catechist Formation*, *Catechist* magazine, and/or *Catechist's Connection*.

## Using the Web

*Publisher Web sites*: The publisher of your religion series might maintain a Web site where you'll find ideas for teaching.

*National Bishops*: The United States Conference of Catholic Bishops produces documents on a variety of topics. Go to www.usccb.org. This site includes movie reviews!

*Rome*: You can contact the Holy See at www.vatican.va. This site will take you to a wealth of information about the Church. Subscribe to a newsletter that comes out almost daily from the Vatican at www.zenit.org/english/subscribe.html.

*Puzzle-makers*: To make word searches, crossword puzzles, and other games for review, go to www.puzzle-maker.com.

*Prayers*: For prayers of the day go to www.universalis.com and www.liturgyhours.org.

For more than 1,000 prayers see www.catholicdoors.com/prayers.

The Irish Jesuits have a popular Web site named "Sacred Space" that guides people through prayer every day. For a spiritual treat, go to www.jesuit.ie/prayer.

See www.dailygospel.org for the daily Scripture readings and a commentary on the gospel from a noted Catholic.

A finger labyrinth can be found at www.the-peace-project.org/fingerlab.html. For a unique labyrinth experience go to www.yfc.co.uk/labyrinth/online.html.

*Bible*: The *New American Bible* can be read at www.usccb.org.

Trying to locate a certain passage or word in the Bible? Go to www.biblegateway.com.

*The Catholic Encyclopedia*: The *Catholic Encyclopedia* can be found at www.NewAdvent.org. Click a letter of the alphabet across the top of the screen or put a term in "Search."

*Tours*: Take a virtual tour of the Holy Land by going to www.ffhl.org/virtualtour.asp. Another tour is available at www.mustardseed.net.

For a tour of St. Peter's Basilica go to www.ewtn.com/gallery.

In 2001, the Pope John Paul II Cultural Center opened in Washington, DC. Visitors use modern technology to explore their faith. See www.jp2cc.org.

Tour our national basilica, the Shrine of the Immaculate Conception in Washington at www.nationalshrine.com.

For an online retreat go to www.creighton.edu.

*Catholic Supersites*

www.catholic.org (Catholic Online)

www.catholicpages.com (Catholic Pages)

www.catholicweb.com (Catholic Web)

www.community.catholic.org

www.monksofadoration.org/directory.html (Catholic Yellow Pages)

---

### Ways to Respond

• Explore the Internet for helpful sites.

• Obtain a copy of the *Catechism of the Catholic Church* and read a section before each lesson you teach.

# 5

# *Planning to Teach*

*Think of your weekly routine.*
*When would be the best time for you*
*to plan your lessons? Why?*

## Planning the Year

Using your manual and the calendar for the school year, plan the lessons you will teach. Make a chart listing the days of class. First cross out any classes that will be devoted to multi-grade activities. Second, designate classes for Advent and Lent preparation. (Your manual might have supplemental lessons in the back for these and other topics.) Then fill in the topics for the rest of the classes.

Depending on the number of sessions available, you might decide to devote two classes to one more challenging lesson or combine two short lessons in one class. You might also rearrange the lessons in the book so that they dovetail with the church year or parish or world events. If you are involved in sacramental preparation, note the days the sacraments are received and set your lessons accordingly.

> ✎ **Tip**
>
> Have an extra textbook on hand for children who forget theirs, but let them know you don't expect them to forget again.

You might also schedule an open house for parents as well as an opportunity for your children to celebrate the sacrament of penance. Your DRE, principal, or coordinator might pre-plan these events.

## Looking Ahead

Look at the table of contents in the book and determine your main topics and themes. Set one or two goals for your class. For instance, if you teach the sacraments in the fifth grade, your goal might be "that my students learn to love and appreciate the Eucharist."

✎ **Tip**

Schedule a special end-of-the-year class in which the students summarize or celebrate all they've learned that year by means of games, songs, a play, or other creative activities.

Jot down ideas and begin to collect items, news articles, pictures, and descriptions of activities that are related to your lessons. Store these in a special box or file.

## Planning Your Schedule

Decide when and where you will prepare your lessons. If you prepare soon after a class, what needs to be finished up or re-taught will be fresh in your mind. You will also have time to mull over (and pray about) the lesson all week. Another benefit of early planning is that if you need to miss a class, your plan is ready to hand to a substitute.

If another teacher has the same grade as you, you might plan times to meet to share ideas. You'll find that two heads are better than one.

## Setting Routines

Doing things in an established way lets lessons run smoothly, reassures children who like the security of routines, and eliminates your having to think of these details for each class. Good classroom management is an essential element of the craft of teaching. Here are some routines and a few suggestions to help you decide how you will carry them out:

## TAKING ATTENDANCE

Either you or your aide can simply check off on the attendance sheet the names of children as they enter the class.

*Alternatives*

**✎ Tip**

Begin class with traditional prayers. This helps the children learn them by heart.

- Print the children's names on shapes (hearts, butterflies, crosses) and put them on the board or a table. As the children enter, they deposit their shape in a box (or move it from an "Out" column on the board to an "In" column).
- Make a large chart, listing the children's names at the beginning of rows. Stick on (or draw) a star after the name of children who are present.
- Take attendance while the children are doing independent work.

## BEGINNING CLASS

Have children put their outerwear in a designated spot. Instruct the children to stand and face the cross for the opening prayer or gather around the prayer corner and offer intercessions.

## PASSING OUT MATERIALS

Appoint a leader for each row or table to distribute the pencils or papers. If the class is small, pass out items yourself. This will be more personal.

*Alternative*

- Have the materials at the children's places before class but in such a way that they will not be tempted to play with them.

## COLLECTING PAPERS

Direct one person in each row or at each table to collect the papers.

*Alternatives*

- Tell the children to give you their paper when they are finished.
- Have the children turn in their work as they leave class.

## GIVING DIRECTIONS

In general, make it a practice to give directions only once to train the children to listen. Then ask if there are any questions. For reference, write the directions also on the board or on poster paper. If you have special needs students, either you or your aide may need to provide additional assistance.

## ASSIGNING HOMEWORK

If you give homework, let the parents know about it through a letter home or via email. Write the assignment on the board or on poster paper and have the children jot it down in their books. Plan for how you will use the homework next time you meet.

At the beginning of each class, either you or an aide can check that the homework was done. You can also comment on it or use it in some other way. Award stickers and other prizes as incentives. You might hold a lottery once in a while. Students who have done homework for a certain number of classes are entitled to put their name in a bag for a drawing on a prize.

## ANSWERING QUESTIONS AND ASKING FOR HELP

Tell the children that they must raise their hand and be called on to answer a question or to get help. Insist that they not call out. In early grades it may take many reminders before the children adhere to this requirement. For students with conditions such as ADHD, this rule can be especially hard to abide by, so it is very important that you be both firm and patient.

## CALLING FOR ATTENTION

In *Sister Act 2* Whoopi Goldberg scraped her fingernails across the blackboard to get the attention of her class. This is not recommended! To get your students' attention during a noisy activity and to end an activity, you might:

- call "Boys and girls"
- ring a bell or blow a whistle
- clap your hands twice
- flick the lights on and off
- play a chord on the piano
- hold up a red card that means "Stop"

- tell the class that when they see you put your hands behind your head, time is up and they are also to put their hands behind their heads (a variation on this is to raise your hand high)
- clap once, and have the children respond with two claps.

ENDING CLASS

Have the children clean up their space and return materials before class is over. Pass out any papers that need to go home and remind the children of their homework. Conclude with a prayer. Stand at the door to say good-bye.

WALKING SOMEWHERE

En route to another room or building, tell the first child a place to stop. Stay near the end of the line to encourage stragglers.

EMERGENCIES

*Fire drills*: See that the children know where to go and that they are to keep strict silence. If a child has a physical disability that affects mobility, you or an aide should assist the student. Be the last to leave the room and make sure that the classroom door is closed. Important: take your attendance book with you to see that all children are accounted for.

*Other disasters*: Just as is done at the public schools in your region, practice for other disasters that may occur.

*Sickness*: When a student is sick, send someone with him or her to the office so the parent or guardian can be called.

*Serious allergies*: If a student has a life-threatening allergy, it is essential that you have written permission and directions from the parent or guardian about what you need to do should there be an allergic reaction and that you are prepared to respond during such an emergency.

TARDINESS

Let the children know you expect them to be on time. Keep track of tardiness. If someone is chronically late, seat him or her near the door so as not to disrupt the class. Don't stop class to find out why the child is tardy but see him or her after class. Try to solve the problem.

## SUBSTITUTES

Determine how you will secure a substitute for days when you are absent. If you are unable to teach a class, try to give advance notice. Provide the substitute with a list of your students' names, a seating chart, and a manual marked with the lesson to be taught. If possible, tell your substitute about your routine activities and special requirements your students might have.

## SNACKS

Snacks are not a good idea because they create messes, attract ants, and cut down on teaching time. The children can survive an hour or so without eating. Class time can be better spent by providing spiritual nourishment!

If you do provide snacks, be aware of children who have allergies to certain foods.

---

### Ways to Respond

Ask other teachers how they conduct routines. Decide on yours.

What routines might you add to those in this chapter?

---

# 6

# The Classroom

*Visualize the ideal classroom.*
*How do you want your teaching space to "feel"?*

The setting for your class can promote or deter learning. Practicing Feng Shui isn't necessary, but neither should the room be declared a national disaster area. Make it as welcoming as possible—even the door, the first thing the students will see. Take time to create an atmosphere that is conducive to thinking and talking about God.

## Religious Atmosphere

The place where you teach the good news is a sacred space. Here are ways to make it a holy place:

- Display the crucifix, religious pictures, and statues.
- Set up a prayer corner and gather around it sometimes for prayer. Cover a table or a stand with a pretty cloth. On it put a Bible, a candle or two, flowers, and religious images.
- Play religious music.
- Light candles.
- Burn incense.
- Have holy water available.

> ✎ **Tip**
>
> Chairs, desks, and tables should be the right size for the children.

## Cleanliness Next to Godliness

Do your best to make the room neat, clean, and attractive. If you are in a borrowed room, you may have to come early to see that the blackboards and floor are clean. Strive for a comfortable order.

Unless doing so would affect students with respiratory conditions, set out citrus rinds or potpourri to scent the air with a fresh, pleasant fragrance.

Leave the room at least as neat as you found it. Tell the students to clean up the space around them. Enlist a few to help you put things away and clean the board.

Graffiti and stray marks should be cleaned immediately; otherwise the problem multiplies.

## Colors

Be sensitive to how colors affect children. Red makes them restless, so avoid a lot of red. Yellow is a happy color, good for charts and worksheets. Orange is energetic. Green is peaceful. Blue is a tranquil color, too, but some shades lead to sleepiness and sadness.

## Seating Arrangement

The children should be seated for optimum learning. If the chairs or desks are not arranged to your liking, move them. Make sure that all children face you as you talk.

The children should have their backs to the windows to minimize distractions and avoid facing the sun.

If your class is not too large, a semicircle of desks works well. So does an open rectangle. Having desks in rows can help with discipline problems. Seating children around tables is good for group work, projects, and discussions. Arrange the seats in different ways for different activities. Sometimes gather the children around you on the floor, move to a different room, or venture outside.

At first, seat the children in alphabetical order to help you learn their names. Later, assign seats according to needs:

- Seat children who have trouble seeing and hearing in front.
- Put latecomers near the door.
- Separate chatterboxes.
- Seat easily distracted children away from the door and windows.

## A Climate for Learning

Be conscious of the climate of your classroom:
- Turn on the lights.
- Know how to regulate the thermostat.
- Open windows when it's stuffy; close them when it's chilly.
- When you're using video equipment, make sure the lights don't shine on the screen.
- Close the door and windows when necessary to keep the room quiet.

## Supplies and Handouts

You may enjoy the luxury of a storage space for supplies in the room where you teach. If not, you might keep your supplies in a basket or dishpan and carry it to class. Make sure you have a few extra of everything.

## Relations with Roommates

If another teacher shares your room, start off on the right foot by writing a letter explaining that you will do your best to keep the room in tiptop condition. Invite him or her to let you know if anything is amiss in the room. If something is damaged while you are in the room, make amends. Stay friendly!

---

### Ways to Respond

• Look at your teaching space carefully. What do you like?
What do you want to change?

• Plan a space for a prayer corner.

---

# 7

# *The First Day*

*It is said that we size up a person during the first twenty seconds we meet them. Think of a time you did this. Did you later change your mind about that person?*

Veteran teachers often say, as the first day goes, so goes the rest of the year. Whether this is true or not, that first class is important, so you will want to prepare a solid lesson, despite the introductions and organizing that has to be done then. Throughout this first class, convey that you have a firm purpose and that everything is under control (even though your legs may be shaking).

The following guidelines will help you make a good first impression and will result in rich dividends later.

## Advance Planning

- Become familiar with the policies of the school or parish program.
- Find out where supplies, equipment, and catechetical resources are kept and the procedure for using them.
- Learn how to run the copy machine and other equipment.

 **Tip**

Some children may try to test you. Be firm and businesslike, but kind. (Veteran school teachers have a saying, "Don't smile until Christmas!")

- Get to know the other teachers.
- Prepare name cards out of stiff paper folded in half. This will help you call the children by name right away and learn their names quickly.
- Put the children's names on their books.

## Twelve Tasks for the First Day

1. Set the children's name cards or badges at their place according to your seating chart. Tell the children to keep them facing you.
2. Greet the children at the door.
3. Be alert to children who have special needs and be prepared to accommodate them.
4. Begin with prayer.
5. Welcome the children. Have your name written on the board and pronounce it. Introduce yourself and tell why you are happy to be teaching the class.
6. Distribute the books, read the title, and have the children page through them.
7. List the main topics of the year.
8. Share your one or two goals and ask the children what they would hope to learn that year.
9. Describe your standards and expectations for the class and state the classroom rules.
10. Explain classroom routines, e.g., taking attendance, collecting papers, completing homework.
11. Introduce the prayer corner.
12. End with prayer.

---

### Ways to Respond
- Plan what you will say to the children about yourself.
- Go over your lesson plan before actually using it.

---

# 8

# Shaping a Lesson Plan

*Do you remember a particular lesson from a teacher
you have had? What was memorable about it?*

As carefully as a producer plans all aspects
of a movie, religion teachers should plan
a lesson. A good religion lesson requires
about two hours of planning. This allows
time to

**Tip**

Aim to be not so
much a sage on the
stage but a guide at
the side.

- get used to the flow of the lesson, so
  there are no awkward pauses
- make the "teacher talk" your own, so you don't have to read it to
  the class
- be creative in adapting the lesson
- use the suggested resources and those in your religious education library
- do the background reading provided for your growth in understanding, and
- avoid unnecessary stress on yourself on the day you teach.

Plan your lessons early so that ideas have time to ripen. Think and
pray over the themes of the lesson all week. Good preparation is a
matter of justice (and prudence!).

## Call on the Holy Spirit

The Holy Spirit is your invisible teaching partner. Before planning a lesson, ask the Holy Spirit to inspire and enlighten you so that you can teach as Jesus did.

## Focus on Fundamentals

Let the lesson's goals and objectives (learning outcomes) guide your choice of activities. Objectives are cognitive, affective, and behavioral—in plain English, for the head, the heart, and the hands. Everything you do in class should further the attainment of these objectives.

## Get a Bird's-eye View

Read the textbook pages of the lesson before you read the manual.

## Plan Purposeful Work

Choose activities with care. Avoid busy-work. For example, making words out of the letters in "Eucharist" does not teach anything relevant. Neither does going through a maze. These kinds of activities are fun for children though, so they might be good activities to send home.

## Think Hamburger!

Every lesson, even a half-lesson, needs three parts like a hamburger. The meat is the main part.

*Top bun*: engages the children and focuses them on the topic

*Beef*: accomplishes the objectives through activities

*Bottom bun*: summarizes the lesson and brings closure to it

In other words, the key to educating is to show the students what you're going to teach them, teach them, and then show them what you've taught them.

## Charting the Course

Annotate your manual as you plan your lesson. Use arrows and stars. Circle things and write notes and keywords. Add post-it notes and clip notes to the page.

Outline your lesson on a large index card and keep it in your manual for easy reference during class. You might use this format:

Objectives:_____

Materials:_____

Process:_____

    1. Opening activity:_____

    2. Other activities:

        a._____

        b._____

        c._____

    3. Summary activity:_____

Homework:_____

_____

Gauge the amount of time each part of the lesson will take and write it in the margin of the card as a guide.

## Three Basic Types of Lessons

### DEVELOPMENT LESSONS

Most lessons are development in which you explain a concept or nurture an attitude. Two types of reasoning lead the students to new insights:

*Deductive.* You begin by stating a general principle and ask the children to give specific examples. (You say: The parable of the Good Samaritan teaches us how to love all people, even our enemies. In what ways did the Good Samaritan show love?)

*Inductive.* You provide examples and ask the children to formulate a general principle. Inductive reasoning is the more challenging of the two. (You say: The Good Samaritan cared for his enemy, bound up his wounds, and paid for his care at the inn. What lesson do you think Jesus was trying to teach us by this?)

## REVIEW LESSONS

In these lessons the children engage in games, exercises, and other activities that reinforce what they have learned.

## CULMINATING LESSONS

At the end of a topic or unit is a culminating lesson, a special experience such as a prayer service, a play, a project, or a celebration.

## Religious Activities

Lesson activities should be religious not secular. The books we read to the children, the crafts, and the lesson topics themselves should differ from the ones used at public schools. Religion is one thing the children won't get there. We need to teach about the faith rather than duplicate secular lessons and activities they already have learned and done. If we don't, who will?

## Draw on Student Experiences

Religious educator Thomas Groome proposed that faith is taught by meshing the students' experiences with the faith story. He calls this "shared praxis." Most lesson plans today incorporate this theory by asking the students to share experiences as the concepts are developed.

Be alert to opportunities to link a concept to something the children are familiar with. For example, to teach that water is an apt symbol for baptism, ask "How has your family used water today?"

## Words, Words, Words

Knowing Catholic vocabulary is a key to understanding our faith. Your manual lists words to be taught in each lesson. Flashcards are a great help for this. The words need to be reviewed at the end of the lesson and periodically by a game or by having volunteers point to a word on the board and define it.

Be aware that some words mean one thing in the secular world and have a very different meaning in theology. The definition in your manual is the religious one.

## Customize the Lesson

Make the lesson in your manual your own. Tailor it to your teaching style and your students' needs. Choose activities that will work with your class, and remember that hands-on or experiential activities have more lasting effects that do passive ones. Bring the lesson to life in the following ways:

### REFER TO EXPERIENCES

Weave descriptions of current events, situations, and people into your lesson when doing so is appropriate. Then your students will see that the class is related to real life—their life—and the world today. In addition, they'll find your lessons more interesting.

Clip and file newspaper and magazine articles that are related to your year's topics. If you teach the commandments and Beatitudes, watch for articles about people who live them today. If your topic is the Old Testament, collect news items about archeological finds in the Holy Land.

### TELL A PERSONAL STORY

If you really want to capture your class's attention, tell a personal story to illustrate a concept. Be careful, though, not to overdo this!

### CONNECT WITH THE CHURCH

Look for opportunities to connect your students with the Church. Know what is going on in your parish (how does it support the orphanage in Mexico?), diocese (what's on the program for the diocesan picnic?), and the universal Church (what is the pope's latest publication?) and then mention these things in class. How do you find out what's happening?

- Read your church bulletin.
- Subscribe to your diocesan newspaper or sign up for your diocesan newsletter on the Web.
- Subscribe to a Catholic periodical and purchase Catholic books.
- Register for the online newsletter that comes out almost daily from the Vatican at www.zenit.org/english/subscribe.html.

Keep students aware of the current seasons and feasts of the Church year. Enter into the prayer and celebrations of the liturgical year.

## Correlate

We learn by relating new knowledge to what we already know. Old facts act as hooks for new information. As you plan a lesson, think of references to previously learned concepts and comparisons that you can make. For example, to teach the concept of grace, compare it to electrical power. To teach about the anointing of the sick, relate it to Jesus' miracles of healing.

## Variety: The Spice

Pack each lesson with a variety of experiences not only to meet the children's different learning styles, but also to hold their interest. Remember that their attention span is not very long. (It's said to match their age; e.g., a five year old has a five-minute attention span.)

- Use the overhead projector or other audio-visual equipment.
- Play a game on the blackboard.
- Put on a skit.
- Play a song to introduce or reinforce a concept.
- Have one or more students teach part of the lesson.

Keep in mind that we remember

    20% of what we hear

    30% of what we see

    50% of what we see and hear

    70% of what we say

    90% of what we do.

## Ways to Read the Book

Decide how you will handle sections of the lesson to be read. Try these ways to vary the reading:

- Call on different students to read sections.
- Read a section yourself.
- Have all the students read a section out loud together.
- Tape record a section and play it for the class.
- Go around the class in order, having each student read one section or one sentence.
- Have a student read a sentence or two, stop, and call on someone to pick up where he or she has left off. The next student does the same.
- Before a long section is read, assign paragraphs to different students. This works well with stories because it doesn't interrupt the flow.
- If a section has speaking parts, assign these to different students.
- Break up a long section and assign one part to each group or row of students to read silently and summarize for the class.
- Have the class read silently. Always give them a reason to read, something in particular to look for.

## Group Work

At times have the students do an activity together in pairs or as a group. Form the groups so that the children work with different classmates. Make sure that your directions are clear. Circulate around the room to see that the children stay on task.

 **Tip**

Tell the students to underline, circle, number, or star important words and concepts as the section is read.

WAYS TO FORM GROUPS

- Decide how many you want in a group. Divide this number into the total number of students. Have the children count off up to the quotient.

Then call the numbers and have the children join the others with the same number.

- Pull as many cards from a deck as you have students, making sure that you have about equal numbers of each suit. Have the children choose a card and form groups according to suits.
- Have the class line up, and then pair off the children from both ends of the line.
- Label index cards with colors (or animals or anything else) and have the children each pick one. Then call all the blues (or lions) together, etc.

WAYS TO CHOOSE LEADERS

You might appoint leaders for each group, or let the groups select their own leaders, or use a more creative way to determine them:

- the child whose birthday is coming up,
- who has the most letters in his or her name,
- who is the tallest, the shortest, the oldest, or the youngest.

## Use Concrete Aids

Jesus, the master teacher, used concrete things to teach—a coin, bread, birds. Concrete things pique children's interest and drive home a lesson. For example, in presenting the parable of the seeds show a packet of them. Holding and touching the object make a further impression, so pass it around the class.

## Surprise

Keep interest at a high level by periodically surprising your students. Be unpredictable. For example, celebrate reaching page 100 by giving the class a fortune cookie with a Scripture quotation inside, or begin your study of the Exodus by coming to class dressed like Moses.

## Add Sparkle with Anecdotes

A speaker or a homilist wins us over by a funny story. Keep your students' attention by telling relevant jokes once in a while. If you don't already have a collection of "religious" jokes, start one. Example: A first-grade teacher wanted her students to understand that Jesus had feelings just as we do, and that he even cried. She asked, "What do you think Jesus did when his good friend Lazarus died?" One child ventured, "Called 911?"

## Counterattack!

Did you know that our memory of something deteriorates the fastest immediately after we've experienced it? That is why it is important to review right after you teach. (That is also why it is a good practice to evaluate your lesson and prepare the next one as soon as possible after class.)

End your lesson with a review. This could be as simple as asking the children for one thing they learned or one idea they most want to remember. You might have them write an ending to these statements: "I realized that…," "I now appreciate…," or "I learned…."

## Over Plan

It's better to have more activities planned for the class than not enough. Always know what you will do if there's time left after you finish a lesson. Play a review game of key terms, ask questions about the year's topics, teach the children a prayer, have them memorize a prayer, take a supplement lesson, hold a short prayer service, read Scripture, or tell a gospel story. Never should children be just talking until dismissal time or be let out early.

## Plan B

Be prepared for surprises such as a guest speaker who doesn't appear or a power outage on the day you plan to show a video. Have an alternate way ready to pres-

 **Tip**

To prevent interruptions make sure that the students go to the bathroom, get a drink of water, and sharpen pencils before or after class. Have extra pencils on hand to replace ones that break.

ent the lesson. Or you might pull out a "freezer plan," an extra lesson plan for just such emergencies. It could be on a topic related to the year's curriculum or one you think the children would benefit from learning about. Also, if a certain activity isn't working with your students, have another one up your sleeve and switch.

## Owning the Plan

After your plan is set, review it several times before the day of class so that you make it your own and teach with warmth, joy, and spontaneity.

---

### Ways to Respond

• Choose a lesson and think of one personal experience, one modern Church fact, and one humorous comment you can insert.

• What do you most want students to remember about this lesson?

---

# 9

# *Teaching a Lesson*

*How many different kinds of classroom activities
can you think of in one minute?
Which ones might work best with your class?*

## Before Your Students Arrive

- Set up all materials and arrange them in the order in which you will use them.
- Have necessary equipment ready.
- On the board put anything needed for the lesson: words, activities, directions, homework, or drawings.
- Check the heating and lighting.

## Before the Lesson Begins

Use the minutes before class for the following:
- Talk with the children to get to know them better.
- Have the children do a worksheet about the previous lesson or leading into the day's lesson.
- Assign a page in the textbook that wasn't used in a previous lesson or that is linked with the day's lesson and needs little introduction.
- Play a song related to the theme of the day's lesson.

- Assign or have the students sign up for parts in a skit, groups, or readings.
- Ask the students to help you prepare part of the lesson: e.g., cut out figures for an overhead show or write information on the board.

## Opening Prayer

Always start class with a prayer. It might be good to routinely invite the children to stand and face your prayer corner for this. You could also light a candle, if fire laws permit. One teacher I know begins class by having everyone say, "Yea, God!"

## Handy References

As you teach, carry your lesson plan outline and manual around with you, or set them somewhere so you can easily refer to them.

## On Your Feet

Teachers should stand during class. Why?
- Standing establishes your role as the authority figure.
- It allows you to see what the students are doing—especially when they don't want you to see!
- It makes for much better discipline.

Move around the room as you teach. Get away from the desk and lectern.

## Attention!

While you are speaking, make sure that all eyes are on you. Likewise, you should be able to see every student's eyes. This means the children are not sitting with their backs to you, working (or doodling) in their books, playing with things, or talking to their neighbors. You need and deserve all their attention. Be silent until you have it.

When you develop a concept, all books should be closed or under the desks, and paper, pencils, markers, and crayons should be put away until they are needed.

As you teach, establish eye contact with the children. That way they will feel that you are speaking personally to them. You will also hold their attention and help forestall behavior problems. When the children seem bored, increase student activity.

Engage the students by directions such as

- "Point to the first word of the story on page 9 so I can see that everyone has the place."
- "See if the person next to you has the right place."
- "Raise your hand if you agree with this."

## Energy

Move through the lesson at a sure, brisk pace. The rate at which you speak (and your tone of voice) can make the difference between bright-eyed students and sleepy ones.

Sitting still and listening or writing for an hour is boring. Have the children actively engaged and out of their seats periodically during class. Add movement to your lesson with these ideas:

- Write or draw on the board or on an overhead transparency.
- Act out a story or role-play a situation.
- Come up and move around flannel-board figures.
- Move their seats for group work or buddy study.
- Gather at the prayer corner for prayer.
- Line up in teams for review questions.
- Use learning stations and move from one activity to another.
- Come to the front to display flashcards or pull questions from a box.
- Erase the board.
- Stand if they think the answer to a question is yes or a statement is true.
- Dance or make gestures to a song.
- Hold the poster/objects that go with your lesson.

Don't do things that the children can do themselves: e.g., take notes on the board, time a game, or turn on the CD player.

**✎ Tip**

Give the children choices in their work. Let them decide the question they want to answer, the color of paper they want to use, and so forth.

## Repeat, Repeat, Repeat!

Someone once said that adults need to hear something seven times before they remember it, but for children it's thirty-four times! To reinforce what was taught in the previous lesson (or to teach absentees for the first time), begin class with a quick review. Ideas: put questions in a box or bag and let children draw them out and answer them; have the children define and erase key words on the board; play "spelling bee" using questions. (See other games in Chapter 23, "Reviewing.")

Make time to review/sum up each lesson at the end of class. This can consist of answering questions at the end of a chapter or summarizing in a sentence (or in four words) what was learned. Assign review activities as homework. Your closing prayer may also serve as a review. For example, "Today we talked about the Good Shepherd. Thank Jesus now in your heart for watching over you and for finding you when you have lost your way."

## Ten Time-Saving Tips

Every second we are with our children in class is precious and meant to be spent teaching and learning religion. Here are ways to be a miser about minutes and encourage your students to remain on task:

1. Have equipment set up and materials distributed before class.

2. If the opening prayer does not begin on time, the children should be engaged in a "bellwork" activity.

3. Start promptly. Once the bell has rung, time should not be spent organizing materials, chatting, or waiting for stragglers.

4. Control the students' (or your!) tendency to go off on a tangent.

5. Be so well prepared that you move smoothly and quickly from activity to activity.

6. Choose lesson activities that best reinforce the focus and teach the objectives.

7. Don't let things disrupt your lesson.

8. Handle discipline problems after class.

9. When an activity has many questions or Scripture references to look up, divide the labor. Assign each to a different student or group to do and then present to the class.

10. Teach up to the very last minute.

## Aids for Digestion

Looking at food does nothing for your health. Similarly just having the students read a page in the book is not enough. We need to help them "chew and digest" the material.

The secret to a good lesson is your presentation of the concepts. A thorough development will nourish your students' faith life. Some ideas for this:

- Your manual gives explanations in terms the children can understand. It provides questions that help the children make the material their own. Use these resources.

- Draw diagrams on the board and refer to those in the book.

- Write important or new terms on the board as you teach.

- Repeat the new concepts in various ways and have the children repeat them.

- Pause periodically to give the children time to think.

- By looking at their faces and questioning the children, check to see if they are "getting it." If they aren't, re-teach in another way!

## Guidelines for Activities

Give clear directions for an activity and not too many at a time. Demonstrate if possible. Make sure the children understand why they are doing it. Challenge them to do their best. If it is a written exercise, correct it in class or make use of it in another way.

Encourage the children to work quickly by
- setting a time limit
- having them stand when they're done or
- offering rewards such as, "The first three children to finish may sign for a part in our play."

While children are doing a quiet, undemanding activity such as drawing, have them multitask by saying a prayer in their hearts— even simply repeating "Jesus"—or by listening to a religious song. When assigning an activity, give the children something to work on if they finish early. For example, "When you are done reading the section, see if you can summarize it in one sentence" or "When you finish the puzzle, try to memorize the Scripture verse at the bottom." Use a song with motions as a transition into a new activity.

## Homework

Unless your school has a policy against it, assign your students something to do before the next class. This could be a page or activity in their books that wasn't used in class, a prayer to memorize, or a project suggested in your manual. The more interesting the homework is, the more likely students are to do it. Be creative!

 **Tip**

Wash a blackboard with a large sponge. Use vertical strokes going from the top of the board to the bottom. Rinse the sponge often to avoid streaks.

If you do assign homework, emphasize that you expect it to be done. At the next class, check (or have an aide check), that the students have completed the assignment. You might inform parents by means of a letter what the homework is for each class. Some religion teachers find it helpful to send home a form on which parents sign (or initial) that the homework was completed.

## Teach with Respect

- Speak politely to your students. Address them as "boys and girls," instead of "you guys," and say "Please" and "Thank you."
- Don't interrupt them when they are speaking or answering a question.
- Never belittle a student's answer.
- Don't take out personal problems on your students.
- Admit when you've made a mistake.
- If you lose control of yourself, apologize. That might be the best lesson you teach that day.
- Listen to the children and gently hold their hearts in your hands.

## Communicating

These statements are "blockers":

"You're wrong."

"You're too young to understand."

"That's not right."

"You'll never get it."

"I don't believe you."

These statements are "builders":

"Help me understand."

"Tell me."

"Please explain."

"Do you mean…?"

When a child is having difficulty doing something, try these expressions:

"Let's do it together."

"Keep trying. Don't give up."

"I'm sure you can figure this out, but if you need help, I'm here."

"I understand how you feel, but I'm sure you can handle this."

"So you made a mistake. What can you learn from it?

## Closing Prayer

End class with a short prayer, ideally one related to the day's lesson.

## After the Lesson

- Put the room back in order. Make sure you don't leave anything behind.

- Review the lesson and consider what went wrong and what went right. Make notes to yourself in the manual or on your plan. How you will improve the lesson the next time you teach it?

- Ask "Did I achieve the objectives of the lesson?" If you can say yes, then you have done your part in providing your students with the comprehensive understanding and love of the faith that is the be-all and end-all of a religion program. If your answer is no, there's a chance to re-teach next week. Know that goals can't always be measured. You might not learn the impact of your teaching on the children until you reach the next life!

---

### Ways to Respond

- Find a lesson in your manual and analyze the steps it uses to develop the concepts presented.

- What kind of lesson is it? Is deductive or inductive reasoning used?

- What kinds of activities might lead the children to understand the concept?

---

# 10

# *Good Discipline*

*Think back on some of the ways your teachers
disciplined you. Were they effective or not? Why?*

Even the most scintillating lesson plan will fail without good discipline in the classroom. Interestingly, the words *discipline* and *disciple* have the same root, a word for "learn." Learning takes discipline and good order. We aim to create an order in the classroom that is conducive to learning. Our goal is to nurture in the students the self-discipline that will enable them to live the Christian way. We do this by exercising a tender tenacity.

## Be Proactive!

Successful classroom management is largely a matter of preventing problems. Discipline depends on several variables.

### THE TEACHER

The teacher is in the strategic position to guide the direction of the class. A teacher who exudes calm confidence and efficiency instantly conveys to the students that there is work to be done and good behavior is expected. The way we walk, stand, speak, and dress clues in the children that we are professionals who mean business.

**✎ Tip**

Important: never
leave your class
unsupervised.

A buddy-buddy relationship with students is unprofessional. We need to be friendly but not familiar, and we need to maintain a certain reserve. Of course, showing favoritism to one or a few students is out of the question.

Speak in a soft but clear and firm voice. Your normal speaking voice will usually work. On the other hand, a voice that is high-pitched, loud, irritating, or monotonous, or the constant repetition of a favorite word or expression ("verbal tics" like "um," "er," and "you know") as well as certain mannerisms are distracting and invite trouble. You can become aware of your idiosyncrasies by asking an experienced teacher to assess your teaching or by videotaping your class.

Be observant. Don't become so tied to the manual, setting up equipment, or fussing with papers that you miss the mischief going on. Try to see the hands and faces of all the students.

• Never teach over the voices and noise of the students.
• Be alert to the children's moods.
• Teach with enthusiasm.
• Let the children know you like them.

THE CLASSROOM

The classroom should be orderly, well-lit, and the right temperature. Seating should be arranged so that the children don't bother one another. Separate children who tend to talk to each other. As much as possible, keep the room free from outside noise and distractions. Pull shades and close blinds when necessary.

THE STUDENTS

Children may act up in class for various reasons. Try to discover what these are as you correct the behavior. Stop trouble as soon as it starts. Never let the children hurt one another either physically or verbally.

## THE FIRST DAY

On the first day impress your students with the importance of religion class and the message that you will do everything possible to see that they learn all they can this year. You will not allow one student or a few to jeopardize the others' learning. Be strong and businesslike instead of overly friendly. Remember, if you lose your class at the outset, it will be difficult and maybe impossible to win them back.

Set forth the classroom rules (or have the children help formulate them). Explain the consequences of not following them. Display these rules all year.

Caution: New and volunteer teachers tend to let children get away with a lot. Do not tolerate nonsense. Set your standards high and keep to them. Remember that you deserve respect.

## THE LESSON

It's said that a well-planned lesson prevents ninety percent of discipline problems. Lessons with varied activities absorb the students' attention so that they don't think of misbehaving. Also, lessons that flow without a pause (while you look for a page or decide what to do next) keep students occupied and attentive.

## THE RULES

Set out a few rules for the class (or ask the students to formulate them). Write these on paper and post them. Point to them when necessary. You might have the students sign a promise to try to keep the class rules. Enforce these rules consistently and fairly.

Determine the consequences of breaking the rules and let the students know what these repercussions are.

*Some Basic Rules*

> Only one person talks at a time.
>
> Show respect for people and property.
>
> Sit on chairs not on desktops, counters, or windowsills.
>
> No eating or chewing gum in class.
>
> No running in the room.

*Avoid expressing directions as a command.* Don't say, "Pick up that paper" but "There's paper on the floor" or even better, "Would you please pick up the paper?"

*Give corrections in a positive way.* Don't say, "Stop talking," but "This activity requires concentration. Let's be quiet."

*The students are working for themselves, not you.* Don't say, "I want you to… " or "I need you to… " but "You'll need to…" or make it cooperative: "We need to…."

## Controlling Discipline

- Secure an aide (a parent, other parishioner, or older student) to sit in on your class and help with discipline.

- Walk around the room as you teach and as the children work.

- If you can't trust your class while your back is turned to write on the board, use the overhead projector.

- Change seats of children who are disruptive because of whom or what they are near.

- Use positive motivation to encourage good behavior: e.g., a row chart with stars or stickers. Make the students want to do what they ought to do.

- To reinforce good behavior, praise the whole or part of the class that acts appropriately.

- Give attention to a student who is doing the right thing and—if possible—ignore those who aren't.

- Don't distribute materials until they are needed.

- If a child is playing with something, have him or her put it on your desk. Promise that after class it will be returned.

> ### ✎ Tip
> Don't bother asking a disruptive child why he or she did something. A young child probably doesn't know why.

## STRATEGIES FOR THOSE CHILDREN WHO MISBEHAVE

There are various means to stop individuals from jeopardizing the learning of the other students.

*Use facial expressions.* Raise your eyebrow instead of the roof. Simply give the misbehaver a stern look, your best teacher glare. Other controlling expressions can send the messages "Stop that," "I'm surprised at you" and "Don't you dare."

Practice these:

- a frown
- a raised eyebrow
- a look of amazement, and
- a look of horror.

*Use gestures* to let a student know you are aware he or she is up to something:

- point to them
- shake your finger
- put your forefinger on your lips
- shake your head
- put your hands on your hips
- point to the rule being broken.

*Use a word or two.* Sometimes just calling a child's name puts a halt to bad behavior. You might also say "Oh, no," "Un-uh," "Quit it," "No," "That's enough," "Excuse me?" or "Is there something wrong?"

As you teach, *change your voice* to signal that something is wrong. Pause or speak:

- more slowly
- more loudly
- more softly, or
- more deliberately.

*Move next to the misbehaving child.* If necessary, tap the desk or put a hand on his or her shoulder. This can be done without a break in your teaching.

> **✎ Tip**
>
> Silence is potent in getting a student or a class under control.

If a child isn't working, stand by him or her and *place your hand on the paper*. If this isn't enough to trigger action, ask, "Is this too hard for you?"

*Don't interrupt a lesson* for one child. Write his or her initials on the board and see the child after class.

*Ignore some bad behaviors*, especially those that are a ploy for attention. This will lead to a halt in the behavior.

*Involve the child in some task* to end the misbehavior: e.g., ask him or her to erase the board or pass out papers.

*Shape behavior* by reinforcing small steps in the right direction and then raising your standards higher.

Know that your strongest discipline technique quickly becomes the norm. Don't resort to it until necessary.

## Punishment

Reflect on what might need to be done. Sometimes your disappointment and displeasure may be punishment enough.

- Never assign religion work as a punishment.
- Especially with younger children, setting the disruptive child apart helps. Have him or her go to a time-out table.
- *Caution*: never punish the whole class for what one or a few have done.

### ✎ Tip

If a child asks to use the bathroom or get a drink and you sense that he or she is not in dire straits, asking "Can you wait?" will usually keep him or her from leaving.

### HARD CASES

Find out more about the student to understand his or her behavior. Remember that "Care is half the cure" (Rabbi Abraham Heschel). Let the child know that if disruptive behavior continues, he or she might have to leave the class for the sake of the other students.

Enlist the aid of your principal or DRE. They may give you good suggestions. Don't wait too long to get help.

A child may be unaware of how often he or she disturbs the class. Give the child a sheet of paper and have him or her make a mark each time he or she interrupts. Award a prize when the number of marks decreases.

✎ **Tip**

If the whole class is out of control, do not yell. Instead walk to your desk, sit down, and pretend to be working. When it is quiet, ask, "Who is ready to learn something now?"

Sometimes a call to parents works wonders. You might also invite parents to a conference. They will help you understand the child and perhaps help solve the problem.

Isolate a disruptive child so that he or she doesn't have an audience.

Send a child accompanied by an aide to the office if necessary. Never let the child walk alone or sit in the hall alone. Don't appeal to higher authority without a significant reason. The more you do this, the more your own authority is eroded.

For a serious offense, have the youngster write a report of what happened and list the pros and cons of the action. Keep records of misbehavior, objectively noting specific acts.

For a child who craves attention, provide opportunities for him or her to get attention by constructive behavior and pay little attention to destructive behavior.

KEEP YOUR COOL

When there's a problem, stay calm and avoid becoming angry. Try to win over, not antagonize, the child. When a student is misbehaving, avoid getting into an argument or a shouting match. (The student might win!) Watch that your personal problems and bad moods don't spill over into your teaching. Remember that a misbehaving student is not against you personally. You simply happen to be the authority figure at that time.

A PRIVATE TALK

Reprimand a child privately so that he or she is not humiliated. Look into his or her eyes; try to maintain a good relationship with the child.

- When meeting with a student, open with a disarming statement such as, "I'm concerned that something's bothering you" or "This isn't like you. What's wrong?"
- State the offense and tell the child you will not allow it for the sake of the class.
- Help the offender reflect on how the misbehavior affects others and what it does to him or her.
- Ask what you can do to help.
- Get the child to accept responsibility for the behavior and cooperatively determine how to make up for it or eliminate it.
- Tell the child what will happen if he or she takes that step.
- Immediately before the next class, remind the student what he or she has decided to do.

## Disciplining with Respect

DOS

- Respond to infractions with quick, fair, and constructive discipline. When serious misbehavior breaks out, end it promptly.
- Be consistent.
- Correct, criticize, or condemn the behavior, not the student. Convey affection for your students even when reprimanding them.
- Focus on solutions.
- Give opportunities for the students to save face. When a student says something disrespectful, delay reacting. Then ask, "I certainly hope I didn't hear what I think I heard."
- In confronting a student, use "I-statements" rather than "you-statements." ("I find it hard to teach when you're…" rather than "You are always….")
- Keep your dignity and defuse dangerous situations.
- Let bygones be bygones.

DON'TS

- Shun yelling, verbal abuse, sarcasm, and jokes at the student's expense.
- Never touch or grab something from a misbehaving student.
- Don't "dare" students.
- Avoid forced confessions and forced apologies.
- Don't make empty threats.

Don't overreact to a minor infraction. Choose your battles. Avoid making a scene for the sake of your ego and your own needs.

## Conflict Resolution

If two children argue or fight, resolve the problem with these steps:

1. One child tells his or her side of the story using "I-statements," expressing feelings and what is wanted. The second child restates what the first said and may ask questions.
2. The second child tells his or her side of the story, and the first child restates it and may ask questions.
3. The children suggest solutions that will help both.
4. They agree on a resolution that
   - is specific, with details spelled out
   - is balanced, so that both share responsibility for making it work
   - is realistic, and
   - solves the problem and addresses the underlying issue.

---

### Ways to Respond

- Practice your "teacher looks" in the mirror.
- Role-play a conflict resolution situation so children can see how it is done.

---

# 11

# *Scripture*

*What does the Bible mean to you?*
*What are your favorite passages about Jesus?*

Scripture is our source for knowledge of Jesus. St. Jerome declared, "Ignorance of Scripture is ignorance of Christ." Moreover, the Bible contains the history of our faith.

Most importantly, it is God's gift to us through which he communicates with us today. Furthermore, educated people are expected to be familiar with the Bible, which has influenced our culture (music, art, literature) and even our language, giving us expressions such as "the patience of Job" and words like "scapegoat."

Suggest that if there is no Bible at home, the parents purchase one. This could be a Christmas gift for the whole family. Sixth, seventh, and eighth graders should have their own copies of the Bible, at least for class. Encourage the children to memorize Scripture verses (see Chapter 15, "Memorization").

## Kinds of Bibles

The Catholic Bible has more books than the Protestant Bible. Catholic Bibles come in various versions. Among these are the *New American* (which is used in the liturgy), the *New Revised Standard Version* (the edition marked "with apocryphal/deuterocanonical books"), and the *New Jerusalem Bible*.

Some Bible stories are not appropriate for children because of their content or language. Choose them with care. Use a children's version of the Bible that adapts the vocabulary to their level. You can paraphrase a Bible passage yourself, write it on a card, and insert it in a Bible so that the children know the words come from "God's Book."

Children love and learn from repetition. Tell Bible stories and pray Bible verses over and over.

## Teach Reverence for Scripture

- Enthrone the Bible. As you teach, have it displayed on a lovely cloth with a candle and flowers near it.
- When you or the children read from the Bible, do so with reverence and awe.
- Have a procession with the Bible and hold prayer services in which the children kiss or bow to it.
- Explain that because the Bible is sacred; they are not to scribble in it, tear pages, or throw it.

## Teach How to Locate a Verse

Don't assume that the children can find verses. Teach them that a verse is like an address. The name of the book is the town, the chapter is the street, and the verse is the house number. Make sure that the children understand that the verses *follow* the chapter number on the page. Familiarize them with the books and their abbreviations. You may want to have on hand a guide to reading Scripture.

## Teach How to Proclaim Scripture

When the Bible is read, have the reader stand and proclaim the words. At the conclusion encourage the reader to say, "The Word of the Lord," and the class to respond, "Thanks be to God." If the gospel is read, the reader should say, "The Gospel of the Lord," and the class should respond, "Praise to you, Lord Jesus Christ."

## Teach How to Pray with Scripture

- Encourage the children to read the Bible at home. Suggest that they begin with a brief prayer to the Holy Spirit.
- In class, say prayers drawn from Scripture.
- Teach the children to memorize Scripture verses and repeat them for prayer.
- Lead the class through a meditation on a Scripture story. Read the story. Help students recreate it in their minds, and then ask questions to guide them into prayer on the story.

## Seven Ways to Present Scripture Stories

Here are creative ways to tell Bible stories either for the first time or to review them.

1. *Use artwork.*
- Do a chalktalk with stick figures (or draw on transparencies for the overhead).
- Show slides, pictures, and posters.
- Give each person a small picture to hold and look at as you talk.
- Use flannel-board figures or cutouts on the overhead.
- Have the children draw a picture or work with clay as you tell the story.
- Draw the story in four parts on a transparency. Cover it with a paper folded in fourths and slit along one fold to the center. Reveal one part at a time by folding up the cover sheet.

2. *Use props.*
- Show or move dolls, stuffed animals, puppets, or pipe-cleaner figures.
- As you tell the story, tear or fold a piece of paper into a figure that has a role in the story. For example, during the story of Jonah, make a whale.
- Give children pictures of people or objects to hold up when mentioned.

- As the story is being told, help children glue pictures to a large sheet of paper, or put the pictures up with magnets.

3. *Tell the story as an interview with another person* (a teacher helper). For example, you might talk to "Cinderella" as she scrubs the floor and tell her about baby Jesus born in poverty. Or you might pretend your cell phone has rung and engage in a conversation with a person to tell the story.

4. *Take the class on a story walk* for a narrative with more than one setting. Examples:

- Go to different parts of the parish grounds to tell the story of the Paschal Mystery: the Upper Room, the Garden of the Agony, Pilate's hall, Calvary, the Garden of the Resurrection.
- As you tell the story of the Good Samaritan, have the children start in one corner of the room where the man is mugged and then move to the other corner where the inn is.

5. *Let the children say a word or perform an action* when they hear a certain word. For example, whenever they hear the word "fish" during the story of the miraculous catch, they say "glub, glub, glub."

You might list on the board some reacting words that match the story and have the children do what they say at the appropriate time. For example, as they listen to the story of Esther, they might say "Boo," when the Haman, the villain, is mentioned and "Yea," when Esther is referred to. You might also have them add sound effects on cue in the same way.

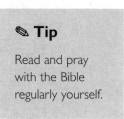

**✎ Tip**

Read and pray with the Bible regularly yourself.

6. *Tell each line of the story with a movement* (echo pantomime). The children repeat the words and the motion after you.

7. *Have the class act out the story.* Videotape it. Use symbols, headbands, costumes, sandwich boards, props, scenery on the board, and sound effects. An excellent resource here is *Gospel Theater for the Whole Community* (Twenty-Third Publications), which contains five-minute plays for ninety-two gospel stories.

## Reading Scripture

- Vary the ways that the children read from Scripture. See page 45 for a list of ideas.
- When a number of Scripture verses are to be read, e.g., sections of the Book of Proverbs, you might write a reference in the corner of handouts or on slips of paper. Distribute the papers to the children and have them look up their verses and take turns reading them aloud.

## After a Scripture Story

Let the children respond in art. For ideas see the list on pages 111–113 in Chapter 20, "Arts and Crafts," for ideas.

Have the children respond in writing. For ideas see the list on pages 120–121 in Chapter 22, "Writing and Other Activities," for ideas.

Reinforce the stories with a related craft, song, book, prayer, or game.

### Ways to Respond

• Use one of the ideas in this chapter and make something to accompany a Scripture story in one of your lessons.

• Recall your favorite story about Jesus and think about ways to share it with those you teach.

# 12

# *Prayer*

*What is your favorite way to pray? How did you learn it?*

Prayer is to our spiritual life as breathing is to our physical life. Theologian Gerard Sloyan once said that the very purpose of religious education is to help people learn to pray.

**✎ Tip**

Invite the children to bring in religious objects for your prayer corner during the year.

## Teach What Prayer Is

The standard definition of prayer is "the raising of the heart and mind to God." Help your children understand that prayer is nothing less awesome than communicating with God. In St. Teresa of Avila's words, "prayer is a conversation with one whom you know loves you." God calls us to a relationship of love. Two people who love each other communicate. They make time for each other. They speak and listen to each other. Sometimes they are content just to be in each other's presence. The same holds true for God and us.

## ASAP: Always Say a Prayer

We learn to pray by praying. Our lessons should be infused with prayer, many forms of prayer. Model spontaneous prayer, for example, when a fire engine siren sounds. Periodically we need to do prayer activities and hold prayer services and celebrations. Ideas for these are probably in your manual. Don't skip them! It could be that the only time your students pray is in your class.

## Models of Prayer

Look to Jesus as a model and teacher of prayer. Point out the occasions when he prayed and what he said about prayer. Share some of your personal experiences with prayer, your successes and failures. Have the children ask other people how they pray. Tell stories about how saints prayed.

TEACH DIFFERENT TYPES OF PRAYER

- Vocal and mental, long and short
- Expressing adoration, thanksgiving, petition, intercession, and contrition
- Individually and with others
- Formal prayers (traditional prayers and prayers of the saints) and informal (spontaneously from the heart)
- To the Trinity
- Asking Mary and the saints to pray for us
- On behalf of the living and for those in purgatory
- Time-honored Catholic traditions: the rosary, the way of the cross, and eucharistic devotions
- Those found in Scripture, particularly the psalms
- Excerpts from the Mass
- Expressed in song (hymns)

## A Few Specific Prayer Forms and Terms

- *Oral prayer* is the type we say out loud, typically with others.
- *Meditation* is a form of prayer in which we reflect silently on God and his actions.

- In *guided meditation* we lead children through a meditation on a gospel story or other topic.
- In *centering prayer* we focus on God dwelling in our hearts and use a special word or phrase to keep us there.
- *Mantras* are words repeated over and over.
- *Litanies* are long prayers composed of various titles (such as those related to Jesus, Mary, or the saints) and a repeated response.
- The *rosary* is prayed by reflecting on the mysteries in Jesus' life while reciting the Hail Mary, Our Father, and Glory Be on beads.
- The *Prayer of Christians* (Divine Office) is the Church's official prayer.
- The *Lord's Prayer* is the prayer Jesus gave us.
- The *Eucharist* is our greatest prayer, the source and summit of our life.

## Set the Scene and Mood for Prayer

Whenever it's prayer time, quiet the children. Gather in a special place, perhaps around your prayer corner. Dim or turn off the lights. Light a candle (use an electric one if safety is an issue). Play soft music. Direct the children to assume a posture conducive to prayer, such as sitting straight (but not uncomfortably so) with feet on the floor and hands open on the lap.

Settle children down by having them

- make the Sign of the Cross lightly on their foreheads over and over until Jesus is in their minds
- listen to silence
- relax
- listen to their heartbeat
- focus on their breathing as you slowly direct "inhale" and "exhale" a few times, or
- focus on a picture or object.

Begin by having the children recall that God is present in the room and in their hearts. Invite the children to imagine that Jesus is sitting next to them as they pray. Ring a bell, sound a gong, or use a drumbeat to begin the prayer period.

## Form Prayer Habits

Teach the children morning and night prayers as well as meal prayers. Emphasize the role of silence for some forms of prayer. Recommend finding a special time and quiet place for prayer. The children might keep a chart at home to motivate their prayers and to help them form the habit of praying.

Let students lead class prayers. Ask the children to bring in favorite prayers to share. Have the children make up prayers and write them. Invite them (never force them) to share their prayers.

Some prayer starters:

- Pass around a box covered with pictures and ask the children to form a prayer based on one of them.
- Let each student hold a candle for a few seconds while the class prays for him or her quietly or aloud.
- To elicit "spontaneous prayer" have the children first write their prayers on a slip of paper.

### ✎ Tip

Small children should be guided to say prayers of praise and thanksgiving, not always petition. They might not understand if they ask God for something and do not receive it. So it is important to explain that God decides whether what we ask for is good for us or not, and says "yes" to what will help us and "no" to what will not.

## Discuss God's Answers

Explain that God sometimes says no because God has a better idea. Sometimes God answers in an unexpected way or at a later time.

## Encourage Journaling

Students might keep a journal to:
- feed their prayer life

- lead them to know what they actually believe, think, like, and do
- challenge them to bring together religion and reality, personal values, and life events
- nourish their personal growth
- heal wounds by letting them recreate hurtful situations and talk them out
- change their self-concept.

Younger children can journal using pictures.

Topics for journaling: family, friends, heroes, dreams, interests, death, past events, Scripture events, news items, imaginary conversations, prayers.

## How to Do It

- Set aside time for journaling. When you do not have time to make an entry, jot down key words on a special calendar.
- Let ideas flow out of your mind and write them down as they come. Let it happen; do not force, control, or edit what you've written.
- Write about the day's experiences and your reactions, or use a starter question, such as "My greatest hope today is...."
- Keep your journal private and be honest.
- Reread it to see how God has spoken to you and acted in your life.
- Thank God for his love and guidance.

## Memorizing Prayers

Traditional prayers are an important part of a child's religious education. Prayers that are memorized are learned for a lifetime. They allow us to pray together and give us words when none of our own will come. These prayers will take on new meaning as the children mature.

Before the children memorize a prayer, teach them the meaning of the words. Have aides or volunteers listen to the children's prayers and practice with them if they are having difficulties.

# Strategies for Teaching Traditional Prayers

*Awards*: Give children a sticker when they can say a prayer correctly without help. Or give them an adhesive name badge on which is written large: "I know the Our Father" (or other prayer).

*Songs*: Use song versions of the prayer in class.

*Prayer Chain*: Children write the Hail Mary (or other prayer) on eight one-inch-wide strips of paper, with each strip a different color. They link the loops in the right order, taping the ends. Provide a guide sheet. Link 1: Hail Mary, full of grace  2: the Lord is with you. 3: Blessed are you among women  4: and blessed is the fruit of your womb, Jesus. 5: Holy Mary, mother of God, 6: pray for us sinners, 7: now and at the hour of our death. 8: Amen.

*Puzzle*: Write the words of a prayer on puzzle pieces and make copies. The children put their puzzles together in order as they say the prayer. Prepare one large class puzzle as a guide.

*Spinner*: Make a large circle on sturdy paper and mark off pie-slice-shaped sections. In each section write a phrase from the prayer. Attach a spinner to the center with a brad. The children turn the spinner, read the phrase pointed to, and recite the next phrase.

*Pie*: Cut out two large circles about nine inches in diameter. Divide one into pie-slice-shaped sections and write phrases from a prayer in order in the sections. Cut a wedge out of the other circle the size of one of the sections. Attach this circle to the whole one with a brad. Have the children turn the top circle to reveal consecutive phrases of the prayer. Or they can turn the top circle at random and see if they can say the phrase that follows the revealed phrase.

*Wind-up Card*: Print phrases in mixed order along the two sides of a card. Print the entire prayer on the back of the card so the children can check their work. Along the sides of the card make a notch next to each phrase. Cut a length of yarn or string that the children wind around the card, going from phrase to phrase in the order of the prayer.

*Banner:* Divide a prayer into phrases and assign each one to a group of children. Have the group print the words on a sheet of paper with crayons or markers and draw symbols or illustrations to go with them. Tape the finished pictures together to make a banner to hang in the room.

*Transparency* (or slide): Make a transparency or slide of a prayer, leaving blanks for some words. Show it using the overhead projector (or computer and large screen) and have the children read it and fill in the blanks.

*Cube:* Have the children bring in a box about the size of a six-inch cube. Give each child copies of the traditional prayers to paste on each side of the cube. The children can keep these boxes in their rooms to help learn the prayers and remember to say them.

*Big Books:* Have the children make a "big book" of a traditional prayer. Help them paste or draw pictures to illustrate the ideas.

*Interpretation:* Direct students to do a line-by-line interpretation of familiar prayers, or do one yourself and share it with them.

*Toss:* Have a beanbag or other soft item tossed from one child to another to determine who recites the next line of a prayer.

*Card Game:* Write the phrases of a prayer on cards of one color and interpretations of the phrases on cards of another color. Show the phrase cards and have the children match them. If you make the cards the size of playing cards, the children can play games such as Fish, Rummy, or Matching. In the card game the prayer phrases are kept in the pack on the table while the other cards are dealt.

| | |
|---|---|
| Our Father | *Loving, kind, forgiving creator* |
| Who art in heaven | *Everlasting place of happiness* |
| Hallowed be thy name | *God's name is holy* |
| Thy kingdom come | *May peace and love be everywhere* |
| Thy will be done | *May everyone do what is good* |
| On earth as it is in heaven | *May we live like the saints* |
| Give us this day our daily bread | *Give us what we need* |

| | |
|---|---|
| And forgive us our trespasses | *Forgive us when we do wrong* |
| As we forgive those who trespass against us | *As we forgive people who hurt us* |
| And lead us not into temptation | *Help us avoid what might make us sin* |
| But deliver us from evil | *Keep us safe* |
| Amen | *Yes* |
| | |
| Hail Mary | *Hello, Mary* |
| Full of grace | *God's life is all through you* |
| The Lord is with you | *God is with you.* |
| Blessed are you among women | *You are very special* |
| And blessed is the fruit of your womb, Jesus | *Your baby is special to God* |
| Holy Mary | *Mary is good and loving* |
| Mother of God | *Mary's Son, Jesus, is God* |
| Pray for us sinners | *Help us to love God as you do* |
| Now, and at the hour of our death | *Today and until our last day on earth* |
| Amen | *I really mean it; yes!* |

---

## Ways to Respond

• Pray for your students, especially those who most need prayer.

• Collect inspirational reflections and stories
to use as a springboard for prayer.

---

# 13

# *Morality*

*What motivates you to be holy?*
*How did you learn to tell right from wrong?*

Christian living is an important component of religion lessons. Our goal is to introduce children to Jesus and his way and awaken in them the desire to live as he did. At times you will directly teach morality in your lessons. You will also teach it whenever you encourage a child to pray, obey, or behave, and when you admonish a child who has hit, vandalized, cheated, stolen, or lied. As you teach what is right and wrong, you form the students' consciences.

*Posters*: Display the Ten Commandments, the Beatitudes, and aspects of Catholic social teaching.

*Role-playing*: Have the children act out scenes in which they have to make a moral decision. Then have the class discuss the options, consequences, responsibilities, motives, Christian principles, and values involved.

*Case studies*: Pose situations in which a moral decision must be made. Have the students discuss a solution, exploring the components listed under "role-playing" above.

*Open-ended stories*: Tell a story in which a decision must be made. Let the students discuss ways to resolve the problem.

*Models*: Collect acts of goodness and heroism reported in the news and use them to illustrate a virtue.

As you deliver a lesson you will also teach a hidden curriculum: certain aspects of Christian morality. You will accomplish this in the way you treat the children, the way you pray, etc. These actions will speak louder than words.

## Tip

**Important:** don't leave a discussion open-ended, but bring in the Christian values.

Let the saints inspire your students to be holy. The children should be familiar with their patron saints and know their name day. Here are creative assignments to enable your students to become friends with the saints.

## Saintly Assignments

ABOUT AN INDIVIDUAL SAINT

- Read a biography of a saint and report on it orally or in writing. The class might hold book chats in small groups. Possible topics:

    How my saint practiced faith, hope, and charity

    The virtue my saint practiced that appeals to me most

    Why my person is a saint

    How my saint can be imitated in today's world

    Who resembles my saint today

    My saint's life

    How my saint is human and holy

    How my saint influenced other people
- Make a booklet for younger children that tells the story of a saint.
- Dress up as a saint and use relevant symbols as accessories.
- Make a puppet or dress a doll to represent a saint.
- Make a symbolic picture for a saint: a stained glass window, a mosaic, or a collage.
- Write a prayer or a hymn to a saint.

- Do research on your baptismal and confirmation patrons, the patron of your parish, patrons of countries, patrons of various occupations, or your favorite saint.
- Design a book jacket and write a blurb for the biography of a saint.
- Write the diary of a saint or a news article about a day in his or her life.
- Write a telegram to a saint and compose a reply, or write a letter from a saint to you.
- Compose a poem for the saint: a ballad, a cinquain, an ode, a diamante, free verse, a rap, a concrete poem where the words form a shape, or an epitaph.
- Create a crest and motto, a tee shirt, or a Web site for a saint.
- Name a saint you would like to meet when you get to heaven. Tell what you would say to the saint and what questions you might ask.
- Write a newspaper article about a saint. This might be an interview with him or her.
- Compile a scrapbook about a particular saint.
- Use a shoebox to make a shrine for a saint or a diorama of his or her life.

ABOUT SAINTS AND SAINTHOOD

- Report on the process of canonization—its history, a cause, the ceremony, titles: servant of God, venerable, blessed (beatification), saint (canonization), doctor, confessor, martyr, etc.
- Create a bulletin board or a poster tracing the presence and influence of the saints through history.
- Collect quotations from saints. Use them to make bookmarks.
- Make a booklet of saints' prayers.
- Prepare a portfolio of portraits of saints (black and white drawings, water color, pastel, and oils). Add brief character descriptions.
- Compare and contrast two saints.

- Design a square for a class quilt about a saint.
- Make a drawing of a saint to add to a class Family Album of Saints or a Gallery of Saints display.
- Put on a play for guests about one of the saints or a few of them. You might use puppets or even just paper cutouts on popsicle sticks.
- Make a saint mobile with symbols for saints that have something in common (e.g., a mobile of the apostles, missionaries, or saints who died when they were teenagers).
- Interview people about their favorite saints.
- Write an illustrated pamphlet called "How to Be a Saint."

**Ways to Respond**

• Think of a moral situation you faced that you might describe to your students.

• Choose a saint to be "patron saint" of your class. Discuss how he or she lived a moral life.

# 14

# Questions

*What "why" questions have you or your children asked that have led to new knowledge? How do children usually respond to the questions you pose?*

Two remarkable teachers used questions to lead their disciples to truth: Jesus and Socrates. Good questions capture and hold children's attention. Generously sprinkle them throughout your teaching. Questions are used to clarify students' thinking, foster discussion, review material, encourage participation, and stimulate reflection.

## Types of Questions

Different types of questions foster various levels of thought. Here is the hierarchy of thinking skills from lowest to highest as identified by Benjamin Bloom. Also included are the kinds of questions or directions that foster each skill.

*Knowledge*: Who? What? When? Where? Define. Identify. Describe. Tell. Recite.

*Comprehension*: Why? Tell in your own words. Describe how you feel. Compare. Contrast. How are these related? Give examples. Summarize.

**✎ Tip**

Give each student a card that has a large "Yes" on one side and "No" on the other. Have the students respond to a question by holding up the card so you see the answer. This technique is good for fast true-false reviews.

*Application*: In what ways can we live this lesson? Demonstrate. How do you do it?

*Analysis*: How? Give reasons. State causes. What are the consequences? Name the steps in the process. Outline. Diagram. How are they related? What do you infer? What are the conditions? What problems might arise? Solve the problem.

*Synthesis*: Create. Design. Think of ways. What if...? How many things are possible? Improve on this. Make a new one.

*Evaluation*: What is good? What is bad? Which do you like? What is most likely? Rate. Judge. Will it work? What do you believe?

Ask questions of all kinds. Frequently ask thought-provoking questions (how and why questions). Use quick questions for review. Ask questions that personally involve the students: "How would you feel if you were David?" Prepare key questions in advance. Avoid spur-of-the-moment questions.

## Guidelines for Asking Questions

1. Ask questions that
   - have a specific purpose
   - are clear and precise
   - are suited to the level of the class, their ability and vocabulary
   - are focused and not too broad.

   *Example*: Not "What do you think about your parish?" but "What activities in your parish do you enjoy?"

2. Avoid questions that are
   - irrelevant or have obvious answers
   - trick questions meant to stump the students or that they can not be expected to answer

- statements without the ending: "Mary was visited by an angel named_____."
- result in a yes or no answer (unless followed by "Why?")

   *Example*: Not "Did Jesus ever show emotion?" but "When did Jesus show emotion?"
- leading questions that halt thinking by compelling the children to conform

*Example:* "Don't you think that the main point of the story is compassion?" "That's not right, is it?"

3. Address the question to the entire group. Don't call someone's name and then ask the question.

4. Do not repeat the question, but insist that the children listen.

5. Do not call on someone right away. Let the class think awhile, at least five seconds.

6. If no one answers, be patient. Allow "think time" for the children to formulate answers.

7. Rephrase the question if necessary.

8. Do not combine two (or much less three!) questions.

9. Avoid calling on just a few children, but distribute questions evenly. Try to call in turn on every member of the class, whether they volunteer to answer or not.

10. Direct simpler questions to students who have a hard time in school.

11. Ask questions that call for the children to repeat important information. This helps retention and memorization.

12. Know what you want for an answer before you ask a question. Your manual might include expected answers.

> ✎ **Tip**
>
> To vary the way you call on children, write their names on index cards. After you ask a question, call on the child whose name is on the top card. After the child answers, put the card on the bottom. If you use this technique several times, shuffle the cards.

## Ways Everyone Can Answer at Once

At times engage all the students in answering a question by giving these directions:

- raise your right hand for yes
- stand if you agree
- thumbs up (e.g., if you can name the sacraments of initiation)
- put your hand on your head (e.g., if you think the father took his son back)
- put your fist in front of you if the answer is yes and put an open hand on your chest if the answer is no
- write the answer to this question
- everyone answer  (If everyone does not respond, repeat the question until they do!)
- turn to your partner and answer the question.

Take a poll on a question and have someone tally the answers on the board.

## Guidelines for Accepting Children's Answers

*Do not repeat the children's answers.* Doing so wastes time and lets the children think that they don't need to speak loudly because you're going to say the answer anyway.

*Respond positively to answers.* Not "You're wrong," but "Nice try." When children are definitely wrong, invite them to reflect more or give them a clue as to the answer.

*Build on a child's answer* and weave it into your presentation.

*Refer to a student's answer later* in the lesson to affirm the child and encourage participation.

*Correct a child's answer* if it is incomplete or inaccurate so that the class doesn't leave with misconceptions.

*Encourage the child to use visuals* when answering (e.g., a diagram, chart, drawing on the board).

## Children's Questions

Students' questions are usually a sign that they are thinking. They can drive your lesson forward and lead to new insights.

When children ask questions, don't be afraid to say, "I don't know, but I'll find out."

Sometimes use a boomerang question: redirect a student's question to the class rather than answering it yourself.

If a student asks a question that distracts you from the planned lesson (intentionally or not), you might comment, "I'll see you after class to answer that," or "If there's time later, we can discuss that."

To elicit questions, have the children write them and submit them for the sake of those who are reluctant to ask a question aloud.

### Ways to Respond

• List three ideas from this chapter that will help you perfect the art of questioning.

• Analyze a lesson from your manual to see what types of questions it includes.

# 15

# *Memorization*

*What is your earliest memory of learning
something religious by heart?
What three things do you consider most important
for your class to memorize?*

St. Cyril of Jerusalem exhorted the elect to engrave the Creed not on parchment but by memory in their hearts. "Memorize" is not a bad word.  Not so long ago religion classes consisted of memorizing the questions and answers in the *Baltimore Catechism.* Although modern catechesis has changed because of educational research, there is still value in having children learn to memorize.

### ✎ Tip

You can practice memorization at many different times; for example, while traveling, exercising, walking, or waiting in a checkout line.

Pope John Paul II pointed out that "the blossoms…of faith and piety do not grow in the desert places of a memoryless catechesis." It's good for children to memorize things like the scarments, prayers from the Mass, traditional prayers, the Ten Commandments, and the names of the apostles because this puts them in touch with the heritage of their faith and builds oneness among the members. As children memorize, they arrive at a deeper understanding of Catholic faith.

Once memorized, key Scripture verses, Jesus' words, psalm verses, and other prayers will run through the children's minds, like the words in the songs of commercials, and lead them into prayer. The words will also surface when the children need them.

Many children actually enjoy memorizing, probably because of the feeling of accomplishment it gives. Just make sure to teach children the meaning of the words and phrases before they memorize them.

*Memory tricks* (mnemonics): An easy way to memorize is to create devices. Make up your own tricks. Sometimes the sillier they are, the easier they are to remember. Here are some samples:

*Acronyms*

- For the regions of the Holy Land north to south (Galilee, Samaria, Judea), think "God sent Jesus."
- For the seven sacraments (Baptism, Eucharist, Confirmation, Holy Orders, Anointing of the Sick, Marriage, Penance), think "Be champ."
- For the twelve apostles (Bartholomew, Andrew, Peter, Philip, Thomas, James the Greater, James the Less, John, Jude, Judas, Simon, Matthew), think "baptjsm" with two p's and 5 j's. (The "j" stands for "i.")
- For the first five books of the Bible (Genesis, Exodus, Leviticus, Numbers, Deuteronomy), think "Ginny eats light noodles daily."
- For the books that are in the Catholic Bible but not the Protestant Bible (Judith, Tobit, Wisdom, Ecclesiasticus, Baruch, 1 and 2 Maccabees), think of the Wild West gang J. T. Web and the 2 McCabes.

*Keywords*

- For the Commandments, teach keywords: 1. pray, 2. name, 3. day, 4. obey, 5. life, 6 and 9. pure, 7 and 10. honest, 8. truthful.
- For the Beatitudes: 1. poor in spirit, 2. mourn, 3. meek, 4. righteousness, 5. mercy, 6. clean of heart, 7. peacemakers, 8. persecuted.

## Ten Tips for Memorizing

1. Reflect on the meaning of the material. Look up unfamiliar words in a dictionary.
2. Repeat the passage aloud.
3. Write it several times.
4. Display the passage where you will see it: on your desk, dresser, or refrigerator.
5. Make up motions to do as you recite the material.
6. Sing the passage to a tune.
7. If the material is long, break it down and memorize one section at a time.
8. Work on memorizing right before you go to bed. For some, this sticks better.
9. Set goals for yourself.
10. Be accountable to another person.

## Helping Children Memorize

- Share the Ten Tips in the previous section with your students.
- Write the material to be memorized on the board. Erase one word or phrase at a time and have the children repeat the passage each time. Continue until all the words are erased and the class is reciting the whole thing by heart.
- Duplicate jigsaw puzzles of the material and have the children race to work them.
- Write sentences on strips of paper and cut them in half. Distribute them and tell the students to find the half that matches theirs and then memorize the sentence.
- Letter, or have the students letter, on index cards the passages to be learned. Keep the cards in a box or special pocket for studying.
- On the board or a transparency, present material that has blanks for key words. Have the class supply the missing words.

- Hold races. Use charts, stickers, stars, and dots to encourage memorizing.
- Have the students throw a ball, beanbag, or stuffed animal to one another. Each student who catches the item recites a chosen verse or adds a word to a passage that is being recited.

## Three Ways to Check Memorization

1. Call on children to recite the material.
2. Have the children write what they have memorized.
3. Ask an aide to listen to each child recite the material.

### Ways to Respond

- Memorize a psalm using some of the methods in this chapter.
- Choose one thing your want children to memorize in your next lesson.

# 16

# *Stories*

*Think of a homily that held your attention because the
priest or deacon told a story.
Do you use stories in your teaching?
In ways ways does, or could, this approach work for you?*

People, especially children, love stories. Our faith and Scripture have
been handed down in the form of stories: the Bible began as oral tradition; Jesus often told stories to teach a point; and, after his resurrection, people told stories about Jesus. When you tell a story in class,
whether your own personal story or a story related to your lesson,
keep these guidelines in mind.

## Preparing a Story
- Choose a story that is geared to the age of your students and
  connected to the lesson's objectives.
- Outline the story in your head.
- Adapt the story to your audience and link it to their lives.
- Use details that make the story real and easy to visualize—but
  not too many.
- Add gestures, facial expressions, and pauses.
- Vary your speed and volume and change your voice for different
  speaking parts.

- Practice telling the story before a mirror and, perhaps, in front of family and friends who can offer you suggestions. You might tape record or videotape yourself.

## Guidelines for Storytelling

Explain new words and difficult concepts before telling the story. Maintain eye contact as you speak. Stimulate the children's imagination by asking questions such as, "See the look on Peter's face when he started sinking in the water."

Ask questions to keep the children on track and to test their comprehension—but not to the extent that the story's flow or mood is broken. If a child interrupts, try to weave his or her contribution into the story. At the end make sure that the children understand the point of the story.

## How to Make a Story Special

Set apart a special place for storytelling—a corner of the room, a storytelling quilt—and gather the children around you for the story. Invite someone to your class to tell a story. Record a story ahead of time and play it for the class. Use props if they are not distracting.

## Reading a Storybook

- Make sure the book is a religious one or related to your religion lesson.
- Read loud enough.
- Use expression.
- Hold the book facing the children and read from the side so they can see the pictures. Otherwise before turning the page, hold the book up and turn it so that all the children can see.
- As you read, ask questions such as "What do you think might happen?"

## Sources for Stories

- The Bible
- Your own life
- The news media
- Books, magazines
- E-mail

> ### Ways to Respond
>
> • Find a story in one of your lessons, perhaps the life of a saint, and practice telling it by heart.
>
> • Devise a "storytelling corner" in your teaching space. What will you use to make it special?

# 17

# Music

*What are your favorite religious songs?*
*Why do you like these songs?*
*How have you used music in your classes?*

Music is an integral part of religion, especially in worship. Like advertisers who utilize music to appeal to people and have them recall their product, so we can use music in our classroom to:

- calm the children as they enter the classroom
- serve as background while the children work or clean up
- introduce a topic
- be or add to celebration
- teach prayer though song
- reinforce the lesson
- be part of a skit or pageant
- tell a story
- set a mood
- add variety to a lesson, and
- build a community spirit.

> ### ✎ Tip
>
> If you are uncomfortable singing for the children, invite someone in to teach a song, but don't deprive the children of this experience.

## Use a Variety of Music

There are many fine religious songs by Christian artists available today. Some songs are specifically for children. Use hymns sung at Mass (your music director can help you with this), or songs recommended in your manual, as well as popular and familiar songs. For instance, during the study of Exodus, let the class sing "Joshua Fought the Battle of Jericho." Don't forget about Gregorian chant.

Become familiar with the songs for religious education by playing them in your car or while you work.

## How to Teach a Song

For small children, you might teach just the chorus of a song.

- Provide a copy of the words or display them.
- Introduce the song and ask the children to listen as you play or sing it.
- Ask a question and have the children listen for the answer.
- Explain any new words or concepts.
- Have the children hum the song as it's played or sung.
- If the song is long or difficult, let them sing one line at a time.
- Have the children sing the whole song.
- Encourage the children to make their song a prayer and to sing with their whole heart.
- Let the class sing the song often throughout the year.

## Song Activities

- To illustrate a point you might use a contemporary, non-religious song especially with older students.
- Have the children sing along to CDs or cassette tapes.
- Let the children clap, click their fingers, or dance to a song.
- Teach the children motions or sign language for a song.
- Write a song for your class or have a student write one.
- Put new words to a well-known song.
- Have a parade or a procession.
- Provide live accompaniment. Play an instrument (or invite someone else to play) as the children sing.
- Have the children accompany a song with rhythm instruments.

*Kazoo*: About an inch from the end of a cardboard tube, punch a hole. Cover the end of the tube (but not the hole) with wax paper held in place by a rubber band. Hum at the opposite end.

*Shaker*: Put rice in a yogurt cup or other small plastic container and tape the lid on.

*Maracas*: Put beans or gravel into a plastic container that has a long neck that will serve as the handle.

*Horn*: Cut one end of a plastic straw on a slant. Blow that end.

*Tambourine*: Take a round aluminum foil pan and punch six holes around the edge. Insert an opened paper clip through each hole and squeeze the bottom of each closed.

*Drum*: Use a coffee can, round ice cream container, or oatmeal box. Seal the lid and tap it with fingers or plastic spoons.

## Dance

The Bible tells how Miriam danced to celebrate the Exodus and David danced before the Ark of the Covenant. Very likely Jesus danced at weddings and other special occasions.

Invite the children to dance, inventing moves as they go to express feelings. For example, they might do the dance of the ten lepers or Miriam's dance. Make sure they have a safe area to move in.

Suggest movements to them. They might sway, shake, turn, move their arms, skip, hop, or bow.

### Ways to Respond

• Find three songs that correlate with your lessons
and teach them to your students.

• Use sung reponses from the Mass for your opening prayer.

# 18

# *Visuals*

*Name a popular movie that teaches a Christian lesson.
What visuals are most helpful to you in being aware of
God's presence? How can you use these in your teaching?*

When most people were illiterate, stained-glass windows, mosaics, and statues taught the faith. Today, thanks to technology, religion teachers have all kinds of visuals at their disposal.

## Bulletin Boards

Bulletin boards can display pictures related to the topic of the lesson or season of the Church year, showcase the children's work, and be interactive. For example, for each good deed done, a child can add a footprint behind a picture of Jesus walking.

If you are not fortunate enough to have a bulletin board, poster board will do, or a tri-fold cardboard display board can be purchased at an office supply store. (An alternative is to string a clothesline or thick yarn across the room and hang figures and paper on it with clothespins.) You may wish to cover the board with a large sheet of paper as background. Compose a creative caption to grab attention. The caption and other words can be neatly lettered on paper, made of letters cut out from paper, formed from store-bought letters, or generated by a computer.

Bulletin boards should be neat, attractive, and balanced. Repeat shapes, textures, and colors to create unity.

Hang pictures with pins or staples. Back them with velour or colored paper (wallpaper, wrapping paper, or construction paper). Use yarn to connect the pictures.

Display student work so it can be easily seen. Do not put one picture on top of another.

## Chalkboard (or White Board)

A board can be a teacher's best friend. If you don't have a board, large sheets of poster paper or newsprint will do. Set these on an easel or tape them to the wall. Make sure you write in large letters and legibly.

Use the board in the following ways:

- Write the goal and main ideas of the lesson on it ahead of time.
- As you teach, write key words, phrases, and statements. Underline and circle words. Connect ideas with lines. Cross out words. Use capital letters and asterisks for emphasis.
- Draw diagrams and pictures. Don't think "I'm no Picasso." The children will love it, and they will feel good realizing they can draw better than you!
- Do a chalk talk. As you tell a story or give an explanation, draw simple figures (stick figures and geometric shapes) to accompany it.
- Record on the board the page numbers of activities and homework.
- Have the students use the blackboard to draw, play games, write answers, and work puzzles.
- Post flashcards, sentence strips, and pictures on the board using masking tape or magnets.

> ✎ **Tips**
>
> Colored chalk is great for emphasis and variety, but it can be harder to wash off.
>
> If chalk squeaks, break it in half.
>
> Write in different directions on the board: sideways, vertically, circular.

## Concrete Items and Demonstrations

Fill your lesson with sensory experiences. For example, to illustrate the concept that a parable has layers of meaning, bring an onion to class and cut it to show the layers. For younger children you might first introduce the item hidden in a box or an apron pocket.

## Flannel Board

The flannel board can be a tool for teaching younger and sometimes older students. A board can be purchased, or you can create your own by wrapping solid-colored flannel or felt over sturdy cardboard.

Figures for the flannel board can be

- purchased
- made by taping a piece of flannel, velour, or sandpaper on the back of any paper figure, including those cut from magazines and coloring books, or
- cut from construction paper rubbed with sandpaper a few times to raise the nap.

Invite the children to use the flannel board. Present the figures as you mention them in the lesson or story.

## Flashcards

Flashcards can be made for a lesson's key words. Using a broad felt-tipped pen of a color that is visible, write the words on white or colored tag board or other heavy paper. Neatly print the words large enough to be read easily. If you have a pocket chart to display flashcards, leave at least an inch of space on the bottom of the cards so they fit into a pocket.

Flashcard strips with guidelines for printing can be purchased as can long flashcard strips for phrases and sentences.

ACTIVITIES WITH FLASHCARDS

- Show each card as you introduce its word or concept during a lesson.

- Place the cards facedown on the chalk ledge or table and show one at a time.
- Ask the class to put flashcards in order (e.g., following the chronology of the parts of the Mass).
- Let the children hold the flashcards as they tell about the word.
- Have the children make their own sets of flashcards for personal study.

## The Internet

Make use of the Internet by finding information for yourself on it. (For helpful sites, see pages 26–27 in Chapter 4, "Resources.") Through a search engine you can locate facts, activities, and clip art for religious education. Also send the children to the Web in a homework assignment or for a special project. Make sure everyone has access to a computer before assigning such homework.

## Overhead Projector

The overhead projector allows you to face the students while you talk, write, or point to the material projected. With the overhead projector and transparencies you can show:
- illustrations for a story as you tell it
- an activity, such as fill in the blanks
- an outline of a lesson
- a diagram or chart
- a quiz.

### MAKING A TRANSPARENCY

Transparencies can be prepared ahead of time or created as you teach. Taping them to frames, even homemade ones, makes them look more professional.

Transparencies require special pens, which come in colors. They can be washed off and dried with a paper towel. For a hand-prepared transparency, use lined paper under it as a guide and write large.

Permanent transparencies can be made on a copier. In this case, special transparencies are needed; regular ones will melt.

Periodically have the children draw or write something on a transparency.

### SHOWING A TRANSPARENCY

Focus the projector on the screen or a wall by turning the appropriate knob and adjusting the movable head. Place the transparency on the glass so the top is by the arm of the projector.

Use a cover sheet to reveal one line or picture at a time. Tape coins to the top of the cover sheet to keep it from falling off as you approach the end of the transparency. You can point to things on the transparency or on the screen. Using a purchased pointer instead of your finger will make you look really professional!

If you want to reuse a transparency for fill-in-the-blank activities, lay a blank one over the transparency so answers can be written on that. Otherwise you can focus the projector on the blackboard, and you or the children can fill in words on the blackboard.

Turn off the projector when it's not in use so the white screen does not glare in the children's eyes. Or you can hang a paper on the head of the projector with tape and—in between transparencies— flip the paper down to cover the light.

Know where the extra bulbs are kept.

### SPECIAL EFFECTS

- Cut out paper figures and move them on the overhead.
- Cut figures out of colored transparencies.
- Use colored transparencies to back figures cut from a sheet of paper.
- Glue colored acetate to transparencies.
- Place objects on the overhead.

- Place water in a glass pan and add food coloring or a fast-dissolving tablet.
- Hold (or rotate) a cut glass bowl or plate above the projector's glass to cast patterns on the screen.

## Pictures

Remember the adage that a picture is worth a thousand words? Pictures can be used to

introduce, illustrate, or review a lesson

show details of the historical period

make an important idea bigger

reinforce a concept

leave an impression

focus attention on the central theme of the lesson

get conversation going

serve as a springboard for prayer

set a religious tone to the classroom.

ACTIVITIES WITH PICTURES

- Display art masterpieces related to your topic.
- Hide a portion of the picture and have the students guess what is hidden.
- Ask students to think of a caption for the picture.
- Cut up pictures to make puzzles.
- Have several pictures of an event and encourage students to put them in order.
- Show a picture of one part of a story and ask the class what happened before and after that scene.
- Have the children act out what is happening in the picture.

✎ **Tips**

Make sure your picture is large and appealing to the children. It should also be theologically and historically correct.

Store magazines so that you have a supply of pictures for activities such as making a collage.

- Take the children to church for a tour of church art.
- Give each child a small picture to look at during a lesson or prayer.
- Have the children write a story or poem about the picture.
- Take or have the students take photos as part of a lesson.

## Be a Picture Collector

Start a file of pictures to dip into when the lesson involves showing a picture of something. Use these pictures even when the lesson doesn't call for them. Laminate the pictures to make them last longer.

## Photos

Post photos of the students in your classroom. You can also use the photos for displays in the church (and school), perhaps even in the church bulletin and on the parish Web site. Photos also enhance an open house. Be sure to request the parents/guardians permission with photo use.

## Posters, Maps, Diagrams, and Charts

Use posters and charts to capture the children's attention and reinforce a lesson. Colorful, beautiful religious posters and charts are available in stores and from religious publishers. Your religion series might come with posters, or you might make your own by copying them from the textbook. (Without permission, this could be a copyright violation.) Here are ways to use a visual:

- display the visual
- show it during a lesson
- use it as a springboard for prayer
- have the children tell about the visual.

### ✎ Tips

Sometimes you may show only a portion of a video, or you might stop a video periodically to discuss what is happening.

Record movies, news, and programs from your TV that are connected with a lesson and show them to the class.

## Slides

Show slides to enhance a study of a topic such as the Holy Land and Rome. Slides also can add to or be the main component of a prayer service. Make your own or purchase sets.

## Videos and DVDs

Choose a video or DVD that is related to your lesson. It should not be simply a time-filler or a substitute for a lesson because you have not prepared. Check how long the program is and make sure you have enough time to present it well to the children.

STEPS FOR USING MOVIES EFFECTIVELY

*Always preview a movie* to make sure it is suitable for your children and effectively teaches or reviews the lesson. Read the guide that comes with it for ideas.

*Have the equipment set up* and ready ahead of time so that you only have to press "play." Know how to work the equipment, in particular how to turn it on and off.

*Introduce the movie:* explain its purpose, teach any vocabulary that may be unfamiliar, prepare the children to view any confusing or disturbing parts, and give them something to look for.

*Make sure that everyone can see the screen* and the lighting is right.

*Have the students take notes* during the video.

*Discuss the movie* afterward.

*Have the children respond to the movie:* summarize it, draw their favorite part, dramatize a part of it, act out situations in which they apply the lesson it teaches, create a poem or composition, or do a worksheet.

---

### Ways to Respond

• Begin a picture collection for the topics you will be covering.

• Make a set of overhead transparencies or flannel-board figures to accompany a lesson.

---

# 19

# *Drama*

*Recall a play you were in and how you felt
about being an actor.
Have you successfully used drama in your religion class?*

Children love to put on plays. Fortunately, plays are a good way to teach. In fact, long ago the faith was passed on by means of miracle plays and mystery plays. Gospel stories, especially those centering on Jesus' miracles and parables, are easily performed. Books of scripts that can be duplicated for the actors are available. The book *Gospel Theater for the Whole Community* (Twenty-Third Publications) has ninety-two gospel events in play form. Your class might put on a play for their parents, another class, or the whole parish.

Avoid putting on a play just for the sake of putting on a play. It must reinforce the lesson and be accompanied by an introduction or follow-up. Also, the play should not consume an exorbitant amount of valuable class time.

## Guidelines for Putting on Plays

*Involve as many children as possible* in the production, even if some just pretend to be trees! Rotate playing major roles so the same children are not always the stars.

*Write each actor's name on the scripts* and highlight (or have the children highlight) all of their parts.

*Make an identification sign,* sandwich board, or headband for each character.

*Use costumes, props, and printed signs* indicating the setting.

*Arrange to have the actors rehearse together* while the rest of the class is engaged in another activity. An assistant might take the group to another room for practice.

*Encourage the actors* to follow these basic acting principles:

- Look up from the scripts as much as possible.
- Speak so as to be heard and understood.
- Avoid having their back to the audience.
- Use expression in interpreting the lines.
- Be creative in adding movements and gestures.

*Have the characters tell who they are* before the play, especially if they are not wearing identification.

*Compliment the players for a job well done.* The group might evaluate their performance.

## FORMS OF PLAYS

*Charades:* Children act out something and the class guesses what it is.

*Cheers:* The students make these up.

*Choral reading:* Material is divided up and marked to be read by solos and groups with directions given for volume and tones of voice.

*Commercials:* Developed by the students, commercials can be very creative, entertaining, and fun.

*Echo pantomime:* Children repeat words and actions of a poem or story one line at a time.

> ✎ **Tip**
>
> Videotape a play and then use it in a lesson the following year.
>
> Costumes can be bought at yard sales and second-hand stores.
>
> You might read a story and have the students act out the parts as you do so.

*Finger plays*: These are popular with small children.

*Improvisation*: Actors perform extemporaneously.

*Mime*: This is a play with no words but only simple actions in slow motion. Silence and facial expressions are key.

*Pageant*: This is a large-scale production of events in scenes or tableaux.

*Press conference*: You or a student pose as a person central to the lesson. The rest of the students are members of the media asking questions.

*Role-play*: Actors spontaneously enact a given situation to solve a problem or gain insights. Discussion follows. The role-play may be done in groups simultaneously.

*Shadow play*: Actors perform (or simply stand) behind a sheet on which light is shone, producing shadows.

*Tableau*: Actors form a picture of an event and freeze in place.

*TV show*: Students imitate a popular show or create their own.

## Puppets

Let a puppet or two help deliver your lesson. You can also use them to act out a story or a situation. One teacher reviewed memorized material by asking the children to help a puppet who got stuck saying the words. Let the children work the puppets too. Shy children find puppets a non-threatening means to speak in a group. Puppets can be purchased or homemade. The children might make their own puppets.

 **Tips**

Your stage could be a large box or a table or desk covered with a sheet.

Paper plates make good puppet faces.

MAKING PUPPETS

They can be made in various ways. For cloth, sew on flannel pieces for features, buttons for eyes, and yarn for hair. For paper and other materials, draw or paste on the features.

- socks, mittens, or towels
- paper cutouts mounted on pencils, rulers, Popsicle sticks, spoons, spatulas, straws, or brooms
- finger puppets made from old gloves or cut from paper so that they can be taped around a finger
- paper bags with the eyes and nose drawn on the bottom of the bag so that the bottom fold becomes the mouth
- paper cups or cardboard tubes with holes on the sides for a thumb and finger
- plastic bottles such as those used for liquid detergent (small ones can be set on your finger; large ones can be set on a newspaper "stick" rolled tightly).
- balloons, clothespins, or light bulbs.

---

### Ways to Respond

• Skim your year's lessons and find where there are plays or where you might insert a play.

• Pick an upcoming lesson and decide how to incorporate a puppet presentation.

---

# 20

# Arts and Crafts

*Think of something you made in school that was precious
to you or worthy of being displayed on the refrigerator.
What crafts have you made with your class,
and what was the result?*

Good arts and crafts neither substitute for lessons nor distract from
them. Instead, such activities reinforce a lesson and bring it home.
Making something engages and delights the children much more
than just listening or reading. Youngsters learn by doing.

Occasionally have your class create an art piece related to the lesson. Because arts and crafts are usually time-consuming, space them
out and do not include too many. You will want to have the material
prepared and organized ahead of time.

## Guidelines for Art Projects
- Show a sample of what the children are to make.
- Write the directions on the board or poster paper.
- Instruct the children on safety in using equipment like staplers.
- Provide smocks or old shirts.
- Supply soapy water, sponges, and towels for clean up.
- Have extra supplies on hand in case of accidents.

- Discuss ideas for the project to stimulate creativity.
- Circulate as the children work, offering suggestions and making positive comments.
- Afterward make sure the children clean up their work area and return supplies.
- Let the children talk about their work.
- Never ask "What is it?" Rather say, "Tell me about this."
- Display the children's work in the school, parish center, or church.
- Avoid having the children simply color pictures all the time. Freehand drawing is more creative and engaging.

## Some Arts and Crafts Projects

Banner
Billboard
Booklet (bound with yarn or staples or using an accordion fold)
Book jacket
Bookmark
Box (decorated with a theme, e.g., Exodus, joy; containing a collection)
Bumper sticker
Button
Calligraphy
Candle
Candle holder
Cartoon
Chain
Children's storybook
Coat of arms
Collage
Comic book
Commemorative stamp
Diorama (art inside of a box on its side, with standing figures and decorated walls)

### ✎ Tips

So that smaller children know which way to place or fold paper, tell them "hamburger" for horizontal and "hot-dog" for vertical.

Templates for art projects can be cut from plastic lids.

Doodle art (while listening to a story)

Doorknob hanger

Dot picture (made from dots of color)

Egg carton craft

Finger-painting

Fingerprint picture (prints from an ink pad with details added in pen)

Flyer

Greeting card

Holy card

Magnet

Mandala

Mask (can be made from a hanger covered by a nylon stocking, with hook at bottom for holding up to the face)

Mobile

Model from clay, dough, aluminum foil, or pipe cleaners

Mosaic (made from magazine pictures, paper punch holes, Easter egg shells, seeds, beans, noodles, rice, or cereal)

Mural

Paper doll

Pennant

Photo album (with captioned pictures)

Photo essay (using photos or pictures)

Place mat

Plaque (coated with shellac)

Portrait

Poster

Quilt (each student makes a square)

Rock paperweight (with felt bottom)

Sculpture (pipe-cleaner, wire, paper, clay, aluminum foil, Styrofoam, papier-mâché)

Scrapbook

Sidewalk art with chalk

Silhouette

Sponge painting

Stabile (stationary sculpture)

Stained-glass window

Torn-paper picture

Triptych (pictures on three panels)

T-shirt

Verses lettered on seashells, wood, or rocks

Water picture on blackboard (it evaporates; no clean-up!)

Web site

Yarn and cloth picture

**✎ Tip**

In your church bulletin ask parishioners to donate odds and ends that could be used for art projects.

## Easy Classroom "Recipes"

**FINGERPAINT**

> 2 cups flour
>
> 2 teaspoons salt
>
> 3 cups cold water
>
> 2 cups hot water
>
> food coloring or powdered tempera

Combine flour, salt, and cold water. Beat until smooth. Add hot water and boil mixture, stirring until clear. Beat until smooth. Mix in color.

**CORNSTARCH FINGERPAINT**

> 3 tablespoons sugar
>
> 1/2 cup cornstarch
>
> 2 cups cold water
>
> food coloring or powdered tempera

Combine sugar, cornstarch, and water. Cook over low heat, stirring until mixture thickens. Let cool. Add coloring.

## POWDERED DETERGENT FINGERPAINT

5 tablespoons liquid tempera paint

1 cup powdered detergent.

1/4 cup water (as necessary)

Stir until creamy.

**✎ Tip**

Add liquid soap to fingerpaint to prevent staining and to make it easier to wash out.

## UNCOOKED MODELING DOUGH

3 cups flour

1 cup salt

1 cup water with coloring

1 tablespoon oil

1 tablespoon alum (a preservative)

Mix dry ingredients. Gradually add water and oil.

## COOKED MODELING DOUGH

1 cup cornstarch

2 cups baking soda

1 1/4 cups water

food coloring or powdered tempera

Combine cornstarch, baking soda, water, and coloring. Cook over medium heat until thick.

## SPARKLING CLAY

1 cup salt

1/2 cup cornstarch

2/3 cup water

food coloring (optional)

Combine ingredients. Cook over medium heat, stirring until thick. Remove from heat. Knead in coloring. Refrigerate.

## UNCOOKED PLAY DOUGH

2 cups flour
1 cup salt
6 teaspoons alum
2 tablespoons salad oil
1 cup water
food coloring or tempera paint
Mix all ingredients.

## STRIP PAPIER-MÂCHÉ

1/3 cup white glue
1/3 cup water
Newspaper

Mix glue and water. Tear newspaper into one-inch by six-inch strips. Brush the mixture on a form, then put on a paper strip. Smooth strip down. Add three to four layers of strips. Let dry for two or three days.

## PAPIER-MÂCHÉ

Crumple newspaper and soak it in water overnight. Tear the paper into pieces and stir with a stick or wooden spoon. Squeeze out water. Make a thick paste with flour, water, and a little salt, then mix with the paper pulp. Mixture is ready when it can be made into a ball that doesn't fall apart. To quicken the drying of papier-mâché objects, make small holes in it.

---

### Ways to Respond

• Skim through your lesson plans and decide on at least one art project you will do this year.

• Using one of the recipes shown here, have your children make crosses.

---

# 21

# *Discussions*

*Think of a good discussion you observed or participated in. What made it worthwhile and interesting?*

Good discussions help students understand concepts, articulate their faith, and grow in appreciating and understanding others. Here are some principles that will make discussions more than "shared ignorance" or time-fillers.

## Class Discussions

1. Good discussion depends on participants' having good information. Prepare your students to discuss by first teaching them about a subject.
2. Write the topic and main discussion points on the board.
3. Set standards for the discussion. You can ask the children what these are. At the end of the discussion, evaluate it using these standards:
   - One person speaks at a time.
   - Speak quietly.
   - Stick to the topic.
   - Respect those who disagree.
   - Don't interrupt.
   - All participate.

4. Set a time limit. Avoid long discussions. Young children get bored and restless quickly.

5. Ask for clarification when needed.

6. Clarify and sum up when appropriate.

7. Don't allow one or two students to monopolize. Establish eye contact with those who have not spoken. Break in with "How do the rest of you feel about this?" or "We have heard a lot from John, what do the rest of you think?" You might ask the talkers to assist you in getting the quiet students to speak more.

8. Promote respect so that no one is embarrassed or put down. Don't allow students to indulge in personal attacks.

9. Gently remind any sidetrackers of the subject at hand.

10. Point out communication patterns: "I think we are getting into the habit of interrupting one another. I suggest we let others finish their statements."

11. Don't be afraid to say, "Could we think a minute?"

12. At the end, praise the students for their efforts.

## Small Discussion Groups

In small group discussions, each person has a better chance of being heard. A small group is also less intimidating for introverts. (See Chapter 8, "Shaping a Lesson Plan" beginning on page 39, for ways to form groups and methods of selecting a leader.) At times you may have to remind the students to use their "quiet voices."

1. See points 1–4 above.

2. Form small groups. Five is the ideal number of members.

3. For each group appoint a leader who will make sure that the group follows the rules and that everyone has a chance to speak. This leader or another person may also give the report.

4. Circulate as the groups discuss, and make helpful comments.

5. At the end have someone from the group stand and give their reports, speaking slowly, loudly, and clearly.

## CHATS

At times you might direct the students to discuss a question by talking to one or two classmates near them.

## INTERVIEW

Have the students ask a partner the question and listen to his or her answer. Then the partner asks the question and listens to the answer.

## BRAINSTORMING

Ask a question, pose a problem, or give a word and have everyone rapidly contribute related ideas while you jot them on the board. Initially, quantity not quality counts. At the end evaluate and rank the ideas. A variation is to give each group a paper on which a different question is written and have students write their answers. Then rotate the papers one or more times so each group adds ideas.

## Other Types of Discussions

*Question box*: One student answers a question drawn from a box, and then other students add to his or her answer.

*Problem solving*: The class discusses real-life situations.

*Fishbowl*: Surrounded by the class, four or five students sit in a circle with one empty chair and discuss a topic. Anyone from the class can sit in the chair and add ideas.

*Panel*: About five students and a chairperson discuss a topic, each presenting some information and personal views. Afterward, the class adds comments.

*Floor talk*: Someone gives a presentation and then the class discusses it.

*Phillipps 66* (or Buzz Session): Groups of six discuss a topic for six minutes. Variations are "Four by Four" and "Five by Five."

> ✎ **Tip**
>
> An interesting activity would be for you to have a debate with yourself on a topic. Change hats or name cards to signify when you are presenting the pros and when you are presenting the cons.

*Roundtable:* Participants discuss a topic freely.

*Debate:* Several students take opposite sides of a question and present their cases for two or three minutes. Then other students comment. Finally the class votes on their position.

*Kineposium:* Students move from station to station, discussing a different question with different people at each station. Cards with station numbers in mixed order are given to each student to direct the movement from station to station so that there is variety in the group and each student visits each station.

---

### Ways to Respond

• Decide what kind of discussions would be best suited for your class, and plan one.

• Use a problem-solving discussion to resolve conflicts between children.

---

# 22

# *Writing and Other Special Activities*

*How do you feel about being a catechist?*
*Write a paragraph or a poem that expresses your feelings.*

Writing is one of the best ways to learn something (and to discover what we really think and believe). Therefore, it is a good idea to sometimes have the children write answers to questions. On tests include an essay question. Occasionally. as part of a lesson or as homework, assign a writing activity in the student book or on a worksheet.

## Creative Writing Projects

| | |
|---|---|
| Acrostic | Booklet |
| Conversation | Character sketch |
| Choral poem | Crossword puzzles |
| Diary | Epitaph |
| Eulogy | Homily |
| Interview | Letter |
| Log | Meditation |
| Modern parable | Newspaper |
| Newspaper article | One-minute reflection |

| | |
|---|---|
| Paraphrase | Paragraph |
| Prayer | Rap |
| Report | Riddle |
| Skit | Speech |
| Story | Summary |
| Telegram | TV show |
| Want ad | Word search |

Poem: can be a ballad, haiku, cinquain, diamante, limerick, lyric, concrete poem, or free verse.

## Learning Stations

Learning stations require a lot of planning but are fun for the children. For a topic, think of five or six activities that take about the same amount of time. For each activity write a set of directions and prepare the necessary materials. Set these up at stations around the room and number each station. Give the children a card with the station numbers written in different orders, making sure that the groups have about the same number of students. Then have the children proceed from station to station according to the numbers on their card. Ring a bell as a signal to change stations.

**Tip**

When giving a writing assignment, first discuss ideas in order to "prime the pump."

## Guest Speakers

You may be a terrific teacher, but it won't hurt to occasionally invite a guest speaker to your class.

- Let your guest know what you expect. A set of prepared questions helps. With your guidance, your students can assist in composing these.
- Make sure your speaker knows the time, the day, and how long he or she is to speak. You might call the day before as a reminder.

- Prepare your class for the speaker so that students show good manners (i.e., address the speaker by his or her title, make the speaker feel welcome, and keep quiet during the presentation).
- Allow for student interaction with the guest at the end of the visit.
- Write, or have the class write, a thank-you note.

## Field Trips

For an unforgettable class, take your students somewhere related to your lessons.

- Prepare them for the adventure by explaining what they will see and how you expect them to behave.
- Secure chaperones to help you. There should be at least one adult for every five children. Give chaperones detailed instructions.
- Arrange for the transportation.
- Inform the parents about the trip, its purpose, required dress, cost, meals, etc.
- Send home permission slips for parents/guardians to sign. These are very important: no field trip should be taken without them. Include a line for information about any medical conditions the child may have.
- Have an alternate plan in place for children who are not allowed to go.
- Bring a first-aid kit.
- Afterward, discuss the experience and, if appropriate, write a thank-you note to the coordinator at the place you visited.

## Contests

Contests motivate students and their families. You might have contests to: fashion a homemade rosary, identify pictures of saints, or draft an essay.

- Clearly specify the directions and requirements for winning.
- Plan one or more good prizes.
- Announce the winners in the parish bulletin.

## Oral Presentations

Individuals or teams of students may present topics to the class. Encourage creativity and use of visuals so these are not boring.

## Visits to Church

When children go to church for Mass, a prayer service, a talk, or a tour, prepare them by discussing church etiquette:
- Blessing ourselves with holy water at the door in memory of our baptism.
- Being quiet out of respect for Jesus present in the Blessed Sacrament.
- Genuflecting on the right knee when entering and leaving the pew and passing before the tabernacle.

## Retreat

Schedule a retreat day (or half day) for your students. This is a time of prayer and activities focused on a topic or theme. A retreat can deepen faith and build community, especially if parents and other parishioners help plan and carry out the retreat.

---

### Ways to Respond

- Plan a field trip for your class based on one of the topics you are teaching this year.
- Make a visit to church to review and practice church etiquette. Then invite children to take a few moments for silent prayer.

---

# 23

# Review and Drill Games

*What review games did you enjoy in school?*
*What kinds of games have you successfully used*
*with your religion class?*

Games are a fun way to reinforce what is learned. A good review game calls for active participation by all the students and provides for much repetition of the concepts being taught.

## Guidelines for Games

- Explain each game clearly and set the ground rules. Ask if there are questions.
- Form groups that play the game so that more children have turns.
- Replay games that the children like.
- Make up your own games and let the children create them, too.

## Favorite Games

*Around the World* (Conductor): One child stands beside another's desk. Ask a question. The first one to slap the desk gets to answer. If correct, that child moves to the next desk. If incorrect, the other child can answer. If he or she is correct, the children switch places. If neither child can answer, the first person moves on. (Variation: Instead of slapping the desk, the children can just say the answer.)

*Ball Toss*: Ask a question then toss a ball (or beanbag) to a person (or group). They answer and then toss the ball back to you. Someone can keep score.

*Quick Thinking*: Write important words on the board. Ask two students to come to the board, then hand each a pointer or a ruler. Give a definition and have the students point to the word defined. The first one to locate the correct word wins a point. Let different students take turns.

*Riddles*: Say "I am thinking of" and give a clue. The children guess the answer.

## Reviews Based on Well-Known Games

*Jeopardy*: Make a grid of five categories that have five or six answers each, ranging from easy to hard. Assign points for each answer corresponding to its difficulty. Write these points on a sheet of paper, and cover the answer with it. Teams each have a noise-maker and may decide on a team name. One team chooses a category and a number of points and supplies the question until they are wrong or stumped. The team that sounds its noisemaker first then may answer. For Final Jeopardy the teams bid and then write the final question to the final answer. (Observers may hum the *Jeopardy* show tune.) The winning team is the one with the most points. (The entire game may be conducted as a PowerPoint program, if you have the equipment.)

*Who Wants to Be a Millionaire?* Prepare questions that have four multiple-choice answers. Select a contestant to answer and accumulate points, paper money, or coins for each correct answer. When stumped, he or she may appeal to the class for an opinion, call on a buddy (lifeline) for help, or have half of the wrong answers removed. Limit these options to one a game.

*Buzzword Bingo:* Have students write words from the lesson or unit on a bingo card grid. As you read a word from the lesson, a student defines it, and all who have it on their card may cover it. The winner is the student who first covers a row down, across, or diagonally, the four corners, or the whole card.

*Twenty Questions:* On the back of each student, tape a file card with the name of a person or thing from the lesson. The students must figure out what is written on them by asking up to twenty questions that can be answered with a yes or no.

*Pictionary:* Write objects from the lesson on slips of paper. Form two teams. A member of each team chooses a slip of paper and draws an item for his or her group while everyone tries to guess what it is. The first group to guess wins the round.

*Tic-Tac-Toe:* Form two teams, O and X. Put a grid on the board with squares numbered from 1 to 9. Have a list of questions for each number. The children take turns choosing a number. A child who answers correctly gets to replace the number with O or X. You might make a grid on the floor with masking tape and have the students stand in place as markers.

*Question Bee:* Two teams line up across from each other. The first question is posed to the first student. If a child answers correctly, he or she remains standing and the next question is asked of the other side. If the child answers incorrectly, he or she sits down and the question goes to the other side. Continue until one child is left standing.

*Baseball:* Draw a diamond on the board. Prepare four sets of questions, divided according to difficulty. Code each set as a single, double, triple, or home run. Form two teams and let the students choose the questions. An incorrect answer is an out. Three outs retire the side.

*Basketball:* Let the children toss a ball into a wastebasket or a box whenever they answer a question correctly for their team. You may tape lines on the floor at different distances away from the basket and match the questions to these lines. The least difficult questions ought to be linked to the line closest to the basket. Let the children choose the type of question they wish.

*Concentration*: Make two of each symbol and glue them to cards with felt on them. Put the cards face down on a flannel board. Whenever a team member gets an answer correct, he or she has a chance to turn over two cards. Matching cards earn a point for the team.

*Charades*: Form two teams and appoint a captain for each. Give the captain of one team a word to act out for the team to guess. Record the time. Do the same for the other team. At the end, the team with the least time taken wins.

> ✎ **Tip**
>
> Mapping ideas is a good way to review. Write a topic and circle it. Children propose ideas related to the topic and write these on spokes coming from the circle. Subtopics for each spoke are added to branches coming from it.

## Puzzles

*Homemade Puzzles*: Make up puzzles using puzzlemaker Web sites such as puzzle-maker.com, awesomeclipartforkids.com, and discoveryschool.com.

*Crossword Puzzles*: Use puzzle-maker.com to help you make crossword puzzles. Variation: make up a puzzle putting in the answers and ask the children to supply the clues.

*Word Searches*: Make word searches. Puzzle-maker.com can help you. Advise the children to circle the word in the list once they have found it. The children might make their own word searches and give them to each other to work.

*Acrostics*: Think of a word essential to the topic and print it vertically. For each letter think of a key word that contains that letter and place blanks going across to represent the other letters. Give the children clues for the words going across and have them fill in the blanks.

*Jigsaw Puzzles*: Cut up a picture from a story that was studied. Have the children piece the puzzle together and tell the story.

## Team Games

*Squares*: Draw a grid of dots in a square, five to a side. Give each team a different color of chalk (or overhead projector marker). When a team gets an answer correct, they may join two dots horizontally or vertically. When they form a square, they mark it as their own and get another turn to answer a question. The team with the most squares wins.

*Stars*: Cut out star shapes (or other shapes) from paper. On the back of each put a piece of masking tape rolled inside out. Form two teams. Ask questions. Each time a child answers correctly, hand him or her a star to tape to the board. The team with the most stars on the board wins.

*Word*: Form two teams. Print letters of a key word like "victory" on two sets of cards. Give each team a set. Dictate questions, alternating teams. As students answer questions correctly, they place a letter on the chalk tray. First team to complete the word wins.

*What's the Answer?* Make a list of questions and put the answers on two identical sets of cards. Give each team a set of answers, one per student. Ask a question and the student on each team who has the correct answer stands and reads it. A miss on either side is recorded by a scorekeeper. The team having the fewest misses wins.

*Chips*: Form two teams. Give each an equal number of chips. Members alternate in scoring. For each error one chip is given to the opposing team. Questions can be on the board or on cards. In turn, the students read the questions and answers.

*Auction Quiz*: At the start each team has twenty points. Each bids on an unknown question. The highest bidder gets the question. If the team fails to answer it, they lose the points they bid. All members can collaborate on the one answer given. The team with the most points left wins.

*Lucky Name*: Have words on the board or on cards. Prepare cards with each child's name and put them in a box face down. When you point to (or display) a word, a student draws a lucky name. That child answers for his or her team and may earn a point. Set this name aside.

*Add-a-Point*: Form two teams. Ask a question. If the first student on Team A answers correctly, he or she receives a point. If answered incorrectly, the first student on Team B answers for two points. If he or she fails to answer correctly, the question returns to the second student of Team A for three points. Set a limit of four points.

*Sixty-Six*: For each correct answer to a question, the team merits eleven points. The first team to score sixty-six wins.

*Double or Nothing*: Form teams. A correct answer earns two points and entitles the student to a chance for a second question at double or nothing. If the second question is answered correctly, the child receives four points. If incorrectly, he or she gets no points for either answer. No one need take a second try.

*Teams*: Form two teams. Ask questions and give a point for a correct answer.

*Art*: Draw something (Indian, a snowman, a flower, dog, etc.) for each team in identical steps as the children answer questions. Each correct answer adds a part, such as an eye, a nose, or a petal. The team who first gets the object drawn completely is the winner.

*Snakes and Ladders*: Draw a grid on the board and mark the rows with arrows to show direction. On the spaces, draw two snakes with their heads higher than their tails. Draw two ladders too. Form two teams and give each a token to move on the board. Let the children answer questions. For each correct answer they roll a die and move that many spaces. If they land on the head of a snake they slide back to the tail. If they land at the foot of the ladder they jump to the top of it. The first team home wins.

# Races

*Row Races*: A person from each row writes at the board all the terms in a given category (e.g., apostles, sacraments) that he or she can. The next person in the row continues the list, and the next, until terms are exhausted or time is called. Each word is a point. A point is deducted for a wrong answer.

*Beat the Clock*: Form two teams and appoint a timekeeper and score-keeper for each. Reveal a list of terms. Each contestant gets thirty seconds to define as many terms as he or she can. Alternate team members. Each correct answer is a point. The team with the most points wins.

*Two-Minute Conversations*: Form teams. The first team is given a topic that must be discussed by the team for two minutes without a pause of more than five seconds. If they succeed in doing this, the team receives a point. The next team gets another topic.

*Two Lines*: The children line up and face you. You define a term for the first pair facing you. The first one to name it wins. Both children go to the end of the line. If both answer together, they have another turn until one wins. Three turns is the limit. Points can be kept.

*Five Hundred*: Form groups of four. Give each group cards that have definitions on one side and the terms on the other. At a signal one student takes a card and holds it with the definition toward himself or herself and the term toward the group (or vice versa). A correct answer scores twenty-five points. Each student takes a turn. The group to reach 500 first calls, "500."

*Finished*: Form groups of five or six. Give the leader of each group a list of questions and answers. At a signal the leader starts with the student to the right and asks a question. When he or she has gone around the group a set number of times, the leader calls, "Finished." Every group stops. The score is the number of correct answers in each group.

*Mile-a-Minute*: Form two teams and list words on the board. At a signal, students from one team choose a word and tell something about it until a minute is up. Then the second team does the same. The team that covers the most words wins.

## Other Games

*Felt Board*: From a box or bag the children pull out a picture connected to the lesson, tell something about the picture, and put it on the board.

*Homemade Quiz*: Have the students each make a ten-point quiz, give it to a classmate to take, and correct it.

*Stump the Experts*: Form a panel of three students. The class poses prepared questions. Choose a new panel when all are stumped twice, or each is wrong twice.

*Free for All*: Pass out questions. One student asks a question. Whoever answers it asks his or her question. The same game can be played with definitions instead of questions. Then the students must state the word defined.

*Grab Bag*: Put questions in a bag. Have the students draw one to answer. Alternative: Use a treasure chest with "yellow coins" (doubloons) for questions.

*Who Am I?* Put into envelopes some pictures of people or things studied, and on the front of each envelope write a clue about what is inside. The child who answers correctly removes the picture.

*Astronaut*: Children line up for the countdown. Each child gets three chances to blast off. When he or she misses or after three turns, the child goes to the launching pad.

*Words*: Give a word. Students write as many words as they can relate to that word.

*Back to the Board*: One child stands with his or her back to the board. You write a term on the board. The class gives clues until the child guesses the term. This can be played with two children at the board at the same time.

*Snap*: Children stand. Go up and down the rows asking questions. Children must answer correctly before three snaps of your fingers or they are required to be seated. Next time around they answer before two snaps. Then before one snap. Winners are those left standing.

*Pass the Hat*: Put questions in a bag. Start the bag on one side of the room and the hat on the other. Play music. When the music stops, have the child with the bag draw out a question and ask the child with the hat to answer.

*Split Sentences*: Pass out cards containing the beginning of sentences to one team and give the other team cards with the ending of the sentences. The first team reads the beginning of a sentence and the second team gives the ending.

*Quiz Master*: Students prepare questions. Form two teams and choose a quiz professor for each. The professor for each team takes turns in asking questions of the opposing team. The team that scores the most points wins.

## Ways to Respond

• Prepare materials for three review games you will try in the next few weeks.

• When you have played the games, reflect on which game the children best responded to, and why.

# 24

# Evaluating

*What do you think is the purpose of report cards
in catechetical classes?
How do you presently evaluate those you teach?*

Socrates said, "The unexamined life is not worth living." This can be paraphrased: "Unevaluated teaching is not worth repeating." Evaluation of our students and ourselves is essential for guiding our future work. Much of this will be informal as we observe what occurs in class.

## Testing

Your program probably includes quizzes and tests. These let you know how well your students are learning and will give you facts on which to base your report card grades and comments.

If you do not have time in class for tests, send them with students as homework or take-home tests.

## Records

It helps to record homework in a record book. This can be simply a check, check minus, or check plus.

Record quiz and test grades so that you know who missed them and also to help you write report cards.

# Report cards

Parents have the right to know how their children are learning. Report cards should be sent home in the middle of the year so that the parents can assist with any problems. In lieu of report cards, you might phone or email the parents. In reports home, always include something positive. Also, state some proof for your evaluation.

## Possible Comments for Report Cards

GENERAL

It was a pleasure to have your child in class.

Obviously enjoys learning about Jesus.

Seems to have grown much in faith this year.

You can be proud of your child's behavior and responses in class.

Shows a love for our faith.

You and your child are to be commended for near-perfect attendance.

A joy to teach.

UNDERSTANDING OF MATERIAL

Shows considerable degree of home participation.

Has a good grasp of faith concepts.

Sometimes surprises me with the depth of his/her thoughts.

Makes a sincere effort to learn about our faith.

Does not seem to be up to the rest of the class, but this may be due to absences.

More help and reinforcement at home would be a help to him/her.

ATTITUDE DURING CLASS

Positive, but quiet.

Cooperative.

Attentive and responsive.

Interested, although sometimes attention wanders.

A negative attitude affects his/her progress in learning about the faith.

Needs to be more serious about religion.

## BEHAVIOR

Is hard-working.

Has a great sense of humor but needs to choose appropriate times to express it.

A highly social nature keeps him/her from completing tasks.

Likes to manage his/her classmates.

Needs to realize that he/she must follow rules.

Is overly active.

Shows leadership qualities.

Is an involved learner.

Frequently engages in unacceptable behavior.

Positive and eager, but sometimes finds it difficult to sit quietly.

Is sensitive to others.

## PARTICIPATION

Contributes regularly to class discussion.

Has good insights.

Usually quite accurate in responses.

Adds much to our class discussions.

Usually must be called upon to participate.

Asks good, thoughtful questions.

Works well with others.

Needs to improve the quality of his/her work.

## ASSIGNMENTS

Does good work in the textbook and in prayer memorization.

Generally completes and is accurate in home assignments.

Home assignments are completed only occasionally.

Needs work on prayers.

## Words to Use with Parents

In speaking to parents it is good to use positive expressions that convey the same idea as the negative ones but in a gentle manner.

| NEGATIVE | POSITIVE |
|---|---|
| Bashful | Reserved |
| Below average | Working at his level |
| Cheats | Depends on others to do his work |
| Disinterested | Complacent, not challenged |
| Help | Cooperation |
| Insolent | Outspoken |
| Lazy | Can do more with effort |
| Mean | Difficulty in getting along |
| Never does the right thing | Can learn to do the right thing |
| Poor work | Below the usual standard |
| Rude | Inconsiderate of others |
| Show-off | Tries to get attention |
| Sloppy | Could do neater work |
| Stubborn | Has an independent streak |
| Time and again | Usually |
| Troublemaker | Disturbs class |
| Uncooperative | Should learn to work with others |
| Wastes time | Could make better use of time |

## Evaluating Yourself

Periodically you might wish to evaluate one of your lessons using this comprehensive form—or you might ask someone to sit in on your class and fill out this form. (Number 1 is for "poor" and 5 is for "excellent.")

| ATMOSPHERE | Poor | | | | Excellent |
|---|---|---|---|---|---|
| Room appearance (attractive, neat) | 1 | 2 | 3 | 4 | 5 |
| Seating conducive to learning | 1 | 2 | 3 | 4 | 5 |
| Comfortable but businesslike feeling | 1 | 2 | 3 | 4 | 5 |
| Students interested | 1 | 2 | 3 | 4 | 5 |

| RELIGION TEACHER | | | | | |
|---|---|---|---|---|---|
| Attitudes of welcoming, respect, love, concern | 1 | 2 | 3 | 4 | 5 |
| Rapport with students | 1 | 2 | 3 | 4 | 5 |

| Knowledge of religious content | 1 | 2 | 3 | 4 | 5 |
| Dignified, professional bearing | 1 | 2 | 3 | 4 | 5 |
| Speech (clear, good volume, pitch, speed) | 1 | 2 | 3 | 4 | 5 |

LESSON

| Objectives clarified and achieved | 1 | 2 | 3 | 4 | 5 |
| Smooth progression of presentation/activities | 1 | 2 | 3 | 4 | 5 |
| Use of audiovisuals (objects, songs, pictures) | 1 | 2 | 3 | 4 | 5 |
| Variety and choice of activities | 1 | 2 | 3 | 4 | 5 |
| Involvement of students | 1 | 2 | 3 | 4 | 5 |
| Development of vocabulary | 1 | 2 | 3 | 4 | 5 |
| Skillful questioning | 1 | 2 | 3 | 4 | 5 |
| Summary at end of lesson | 1 | 2 | 3 | 4 | 5 |
| Meaningful homework | 1 | 2 | 3 | 4 | 5 |
| Evaluation | 1 | 2 | 3 | 4 | 5 |

CATHOLIC FAITH COMPONENTS

| Religious symbols/prayer corner | 1 | 2 | 3 | 4 | 5 |
| Integration of prayer | 1 | 2 | 3 | 4 | 5 |
| Correlation of faith with students' experiences | 1 | 2 | 3 | 4 | 5 |
| References to church, parish life today | 1 | 2 | 3 | 4 | 5 |
| Religion teacher's personal witness | 1 | 2 | 3 | 4 | 5 |
| Challenge to live an aspect of the faith | 1 | 2 | 3 | 4 | 5 |

CLASSROOM MANAGEMENT

| Orderly routines | 1 | 2 | 3 | 4 | 5 |
| Economical use of time | 1 | 2 | 3 | 4 | 5 |
| Motivation of students | 1 | 2 | 3 | 4 | 5 |
| Prevention of discipline problems | 1 | 2 | 3 | 4 | 5 |
| Handling of discipline problems | 1 | 2 | 3 | 4 | 5 |
| Holding attention | 1 | 2 | 3 | 4 | 5 |
| Provision for individual differences | 1 | 2 | 3 | 4 | 5 |
| Setting standards for students | 1 | 2 | 3 | 4 | 5 |

COMMENTS: _____

_____

## End-of the-year Evaluation

When the year of teaching is over, look back over your lessons and ask these questions:

- What went right?
- What went wrong?
- How will I improve the next time I teach?

### Ways to Respond

- Write a resolution to evaluate yourself this year using a particular method.

- Did your evaluation of the children improve their participation, behavior, and so on? If not, what might you do about this?

# 25

# *Parents and Other Allies*

*Recall when you have been a mentor for someone
or when someone has mentored you.
What has been your experience of working with parents?*

You are not alone in this grand, demanding work of teaching the gospel. Here are some coworkers and what they can do for you if you ask them.

## The Holy Spirit

The Spirit of Jesus is teacher and counselor, sent to guide and enlighten the Church. Pray to the Holy Spirit as you plan your lessons and before you walk through the door of your classroom. Ask the Spirit to open the minds and hearts of your students.

## Parents

Your chief and best coworkers are the parents of your students. Write them an introductory letter in which you tell about yourself and your hopes for the class. Welcome them to visit your classroom whenever they wish.

**Tip**

Send postcards to parents commenting on their children's progress or send "telegrams" home with the children.

Get to know the parents through informal conversation before and after class and at parish events. You have a stronger influence over students when they are aware you know their parents.

Enlist parents' help whenever you can and remember to write them a thank-you note. Use a newsletter, phone calls, email, and parent conferences to keep them apprised of what is happening in your class and how their children are doing. Call a parent conference whenever you feel it is necessary. Working with parents involves them in faith formation, which is the primary focus of catechesis.

## Ten Ways to Get the Good News Home

1. Homework
   - At the beginning of each month, send home a list of the assignments. Require parents to sign a form or the homework itself when it is finished.
   - Periodically give parents a homework assignment related to a lesson.
   - Assign homework that calls for the children to interact with their parents.
   - Have the children bring objects from home to class.
   - Direct the children to tell their parents about something done in class.
2. Invitations
   - Invite the parents and grandparents to the class for an open house with special activities such as a play, a prayer service, and review games.
   - Invite family members to be guest speakers.
   - Ask family members to help with class projects, field trips, or service projects.

3. Flyers about Family Projects
   - Send home flyers with ideas for family projects such as: developing a family coat of arms and motto, choosing a patron saint, telling the stories of their own patron saints, watching a TV program together and discussing it, finding ways to celebrate Sunday together, visiting different churches during the summer, making a mobile, writing a family prayer, creed, or mission statement.
4. Family Meetings
   - Call the families together for meetings or workshops that take the form of a lecture, a media presentation, prayer services, small group discussions, and activities. The meetings could center around a project for the parish community or for the needy. Provide something to take home as a reminder of the theme of the evening.
   - Hold family nights that include a simple meal, a prayer, a talk on a topic, and a craft done together. Advent and Lent are good times for this. The families could create a project that will help them observe the season.
   - Survey what the parents' needs and interests are.
5. Objects from Classes
   Send home objects to be displayed or discussed:
   - Bookmarks with a quote linked to a lesson, a list of the seven sacraments, a prayer.
   - Children's papers or artwork that have been laminated.
   - Small religious artwork backed by a strip of magnet.
   - A booklet of all the children's work circulated among the families.
   - Art framed by construction paper or a computer-generated border.
   - A videotape of a play, a prayer service, or role-playing sessions.

6. Parent Letters
   - Periodically send home letters to the parents. Tell about a lesson or a class project. Ask for supplies: empty tissue boxes, holy cards, etc. If possible, put out a monthly newsletter. Have the children write letters to their parents telling what they learned.
7. Share Books
   - Lend books to parents. Let them know the titles of books that would help their children. Suggest that they buy these for their children as a Christmas gift or for their birthdays.
8. Prayer
   - Invite parents to the children's celebration of the sacrament of reconciliation or a special prayer service.
   - Ask the parents for special intentions to include in the class prayers.
   - Let each child make a paper chain with the name of a classmate on each link. Each day of class they remove one, and they and their family pray for that child or that child's intentions.
   - Send home a few rosaries in May and October and have the families each pray a decade for the class intentions. Have families make a unique rosary.
   - Compose a class prayer and send it home for families to pray.
   - Have the children take turns taking home a statue of the Blessed Mother and invite their family to pray to Mary during the week.
   - Involve the children in the services for religious feasts, such as Passion (Palm) Sunday and the Easter Triduum. This will draw parents to the celebrations.
9. Songs and Stories
   - Teach the children religious songs, which they then will be singing at home. Encourage the children to incorporate family stories into the lessons. Have them bring in photos of their baptism, their parents' wedding, or their vacations and tell the stories.

10. Lectures and Workshops
    - Provide lectures and workshops that will help parents grow in faith and bring up their children in the faith.

## Parallel Teachers

Two heads are better than one. If possible, meet with the teacher or teachers who have the same grade as you. Plan your lessons together or at least swap ideas. From time to time you might combine classes for a lesson.

## Fellow Teachers

Ask other religion teachers for help and for their ideas. Offer them your support too and sympathy if necessary.

## Aides

Aides are invaluable because they help you with maintaining discipline, preparing materials, and performing routine chores. To maximize the benefit of their presence in your classroom, make sure they understand exactly what you expect of them. Express your appreciation verbally and perhaps by a small gift.

## Administrators

The director of religious education, the principal, and any coordinators are responsible for running the program smoothly. Draw on their expertise in the faith and in teaching. Support them by cooperating with them and by participating in activities they plan.

## Priests and Deacons

The clergy at your parish are also teachers. Make sure your children know who they are. Invite them to your class to teach a lesson or talk. Have the children send them cards and letters.

## Parishioners

It takes a whole parish to catechize our children. Involve individual parishioners as much as you can in your lessons. Invite them in to talk or to help with an art activity. Choose some to be prayer partners for your children.

### Ways to Respond

• Get the phone numbers and e-mail addresses of the parents and parishioners who might be able to help you during the year.

• Plan a family-day class and have children share what they are learning with their parents and siblings. Invite other members of the parish as well.

# A Final Word

Michael Warren, professor of theology and catechetical ministry at St. John's University in New York, describes our ministry well: "Catechesis is a smiling invitation to join the gospel's dance, a dance not of one's arrival but of one's way forward, toward the unnamable and unforgettable."

Remember that you do not have to do it all. Your students will learn things in future classes. Impress them with how much there is to know about God and our faith. In this way you will plant the seeds for adult education.

If you do not feel successful as a religion teacher, do not become discouraged. It may be that your busy life does not allow you to do justice to the ministry of catechesis. Or perhaps your are more suited to another grade level. Otherwise, trust that somehow God is using you to build the kingdom in ways you may never know on this earth.

# Prayer of a Religion Teacher

O loving God,
  my creator, my savior, and my sanctifier,
  how blessed I am to know you and your love.
Help me share this faith with others
  by teaching as Jesus did.
Give me the insight to translate
  the great mysteries of faith to my students
    so that their minds can grasp them.
Give me the enthusiasm
  to convey your incredible love
  by my words and actions
    so that it sets their hearts aflame.
Then together someday
  may we all be one with you,
  wrapped in your love
  and singing your glory forever.
Amen.